MW00990077

STREAMS OF HISTORY

ANCIENT ROME

STREAMS OF HISTORY
ANCIENT ROME

BY

ELLWOOD W. KEMP

EDITED BY

LISA M. RIPPERTON

YESTERDAY'S CLASSICS

CHAPEL HILL, NORTH CAROLINA

This edition, first published in 2008 by Yesterday's Classics, an imprint of Yesterday's Classics, LLC, is an edited excerpt from a work originally published by Ginn and Company in 1902. For the complete listing of the books that are published by Yesterday's Classics, please visit www.yesterdaysclassics.com. Yesterday's Classics is the publishing arm of the Baldwin Online Children's Literature Project which presents the complete text of hundreds of classic books for children at www.mainlesson.com.

ISBN-10: 1-59915-256-8

ISBN-13: 978-1-59915-256-1

Yesterday's Classics, LLC
PO Box 3418
Chapel Hill, NC 27515

CONTENTS

THE GEOGRAPHY OF ITALY

IF you will take a glance at the map of Europe, you will see that not very far west of Greece, extending seven hundred miles down into the Mediterranean Sea, is a slender peninsula which looks very much like a great boot. It seems to have its back turned toward the back of Greece and is drawn up to kick, as if it were a ball, the little island which you see near it. This peninsula is Italy, and the island is Sicily, but it is mostly of the peninsula that we wish first to learn.

Italy extends far out into the sea, and seems to be almost in the center of it. Westward, at no very great distance, lies the peninsula of Spain. Eastward, and scarcely farther away than Spain, are Egypt and the lands of the Phœnicians and of the Jews. Greece is so near, that standing on the eastern shore of Italy on a bright, clear day, one can see the dim outlines of its western coast; and Africa is only a few hours sail to the south. Any one of these countries can be reached easily and quickly from Italy. In fact, Italy is the central country of the Mediterranean Sea.

Italy differs greatly from Greece in shape. Greece is made up of a large peninsula, which in turn consists of many smaller ones. On a map it looks somewhat like a maple leaf, being cut up into many narrow, sharp points, or like a palm to which are attached the stubby fingers.

Italy is not so. It is of an average width of about one hundred miles at all places except in the north, and has only a few sharp projections. Since the whole peninsula is shaped like a boot, one of the projections may be called the toe; another looks like a rather high heel; the third one, on its back, if it were only lower down, would look very much like a spur on the heel.

You may think of Italy in general as being about once the width, twice the length, and twice the extent of Florida. As I have already told you, scarcely any part of it is more than a hundred miles wide, and it is only six or seven times as long as wide. At its northern end, where it spreads out into the high top of the boot, and is really no longer a peninsula, it becomes about three times as wide as before. Its northern boundary is formed by the high and rugged Alps, which extend in a kind of half-circle from the Mediterranean to the Adriatic Sea, thus, like a mighty wall, shutting Italy off to a great extent from the rest of the continent. Through these mountains there are very few passes, and even these are very rugged and difficult to cross, for they are filled with deep snows and large glaciers. Italy thus formed in ancient times a kind of out-of-the-way place, in which her greatest city, Rome, developed without much interference from the barbarians of the North.

Most of this wider part of Italy just south of the Alps (now called the Plain of Lombardy) forms a level expanse about as large as Indiana. It is the richest part of all Italy. The melting snows of the Alps start many streams, which flow down the mountain sides and unite to form the River Po, which flows eastward through the plains and empties into the Adriatic Sea. The little streams that come tumbling down the mountain side are very swift and carry down a large amount of rich soil. This soil, being washed down into the plain below and spread out over the valley, makes the Po valley very productive.

If we should go there today, we should find great fields of waving grain and large groves of mulberry trees. On the Adriatic, north of the mouth of the Po, the interesting city of Venice now stands on more than a hundred little islands, and the gondolas sail on its streets of water, arched over by hundreds of bridges. But long ago, when Rome was beginning to rise, there was no Venice, and on the plain there were but few fields of grain and groves of mulberry trees. Here, where now all is so beautiful, were then only large, unhealthy marshes and many low sandy islands, —the homes of a few scattered fishermen. Through these islands and swamps the dirty waters of the Po found their way slowly to the sea in many shallow mouths. Thus, because of the swamps and the absence of good harbors, northern Italy did not have great cities grow up in it in early times.

On the south side of the northern plain, beginning where the Alps meet the Mediterranean, starts another great chain of mountains. At first they so closely follow the shore that a road can barely creep between the foothills and the sea. These mountains run at first eastward till they almost cross the peninsula, and then, bending southward, continue throughout the length of Italy, making a backbone for the country. Down into the toe of the boot they extend, and, at last, reaching the sea, jump over the strait into the island of Sicily. These are the Apennines. They do not have the many pointed peaks, nor are they so high, as the rugged and snowy Alps. Their sides, even to the very top, are covered with fine forests of oak, elm, pine and chestnut, thus giving plenty of timber for building ships. Rome found these forests of great value when she came to build a navy with which to fight the Carthaginians on the sea.

You must thus imagine Italy as having had a belt through its center from north to south, bristling with mountain chains and peaks, through which, however, were many easy passes, and on both sides of which were hilly plains, sloping down to the sea. Between the chains, among the peaks, and along the mountain sides, lay many valleys in which herds of long horned cattle and large flocks of sheep, herded by men who loved a rough mountain life, found excellent pastures.

The eastern slope of Italy is short and steep, and so rugged that it is only fitted for people who can live on the products of a shepherd's life. There are few harbors on the coast, and there is little to invite people who are seeking homes. For this reason, as I have already said, it was the back of Italy which was turned toward Greece and the east. On the west side of the mountains the slope is gentler, and contains several quite large fertile plains where grains may be raised; and in the south, near the toe, the climate is so mild that tropical fruits, such as the olive, the orange and the fig, are found in great abundance. Grape vines grow in great numbers, and climbing to the very tops of the trees, produce large quantities of fruit. The western coast contains several good harbors. Thus the face of Italy may be said to be turned toward Spain and the west.

Since the peninsula is so narrow and the distance from the Apennines to the sea is not great, you must not expect to find long, deep rivers, none even so large as the Po. Indeed they are very much like those of Greece,—short, rapid, and overflowing during the rains or at the time when the hot sun melts the snow on the mountain tops, and only small and dried up at other times. There is but one river on which even a boat of considerable size can sail. This is the Tiber, which rises in the Apennines where they bend south into the peninsula, and then flows south about one hundred eighty-five miles, emptying through a small plain into the Mediterranean about halfway down the peninsula. It will carry boats over about fifty miles of its lower course.

The plain through which it flows is the largest one on this slope and is called Latium. It was on the banks of the Tiber and in this plain that the most interesting life of Italy developed; for here, on a low group of hills, fifteen miles from the mouth of the Tiber, grew up Rome,—the mighty center of the ancient world. Although Rome began with rude huts for homes and with a mud wall, the people learned to make use of the things around them until this city grew to be wealthy, and finally master of all Italy, and then of every country touching the Mediterranean.

Out over a plain not larger than an average western county, Rome slowly spread, during a period of three hundred years, learning all the time how to govern the various peoples who lived in the lowlands. Having learned this lesson of how to govern herself, she spent the next two hundred years in conquering the highlanders—the rude people who lived up in the mountain valleys—and teaching them the lessons of law and order.

Near the seashore, throughout the plain of Latium, were many marshes much like those near the mouth of the Po. These in the hot Italian sun became full of malaria, and the people who braved the danger of fever had to build great drains before the country became healthy. The waters of "Yellow Tiber," filled with mud swept down from the mountain side, could not be used for drinking and bathing, so the people constructed waterways—aqueducts, they called them—from the pure mountain springs miles away, to bring water to the city. This taught them how to build arches in tunneling the mountains and bridging the rivers and valleys.

The mountains were filled with white limestone, which, if placed in the air, became hard and took on beautiful tints. This they used for building their temples and other fine buildings, for near Rome there was no marble as there was near Athens. From the old volcanoes, too, they obtained great quantities of lava, which they used in building roads so well that some of them remain at the present day.

But all this required hundreds of years of work, and the people who patiently did these things, in thus learning to rule nature, learned at the same time to rule men. Rome's last great work in history was to overcome all the peoples around the Mediterranean Sea, and to teach them her great lessons of law and order. This she had no great trouble in doing, for being in the very center of the Mediterranean, and having wonderful power for governing people, she had but to reach her mighty arms to the east and the west and bind them all together at the one common center—Rome—through the great lessons of industry and law which she taught so well to those whom she overcame, that they were never forgotten.

ROME IN HER INFANCY

WHILE we were watching Greece win her freedom on the fields of Marathon and Platæa, and while we followed Alexander into the far East, where he carried Grecian arms and culture, and while the Egyptians at Alexandria were taking up Grecian thought and carrying it back to the land of the Nile, there was growing up on the banks of the Tiber a city which became, because of what it did, the greatest city of the world.

It was, perhaps, a very fortunate thing for Rome that these other great peoples had affairs of their own, so that she was left undisturbed to grow slowly, as all great and lasting nations must grow.

But before we go on to study about Rome, let us recall to mind the most important facts about the country surrounding Rome. Only two or three days' travel by trireme westward from the beautiful island-fringed Greece, and almost in the very middle of the blue Mediterranean, is where the people lived whom we are to study about now. We might, as I have already told you, call the country the "Boot Country," for it resembles a great boot, looking as if it were hung out into the water, and fastened by the upper, or northern, end. Look at the map and see what a long coast line this gives Italy, and how friend and foe alike could reach her by water. This fact may lead Rome to become a trading people, and it may finally lead her to go out to the peoples around the Mediterranean to conquer and to rule them. You notice that Italy is not cut to pieces as is Greece by arms of the sea extending far into the land, nor are there numerous islands scattered around her coasts; nor do her mountains, which have good passes, serve to divide the country into small sections, so much as do those of Greece. Thus, because the country is comparatively united, the people tend to become more united.

The eastern coast has no good harbors, and people would seldom enter to trade from that side; but the western coast has several good harbors and fertile plains, and it is from this side that Italy invites people to enter.

We shall sail into the best harbor along the coast. It is the harbor of the Tiber, which leads us into a beautiful plain, where the sky is bluer and the climate pleasanter than even in Greece, if such a thing were possible.

Overlooking this beautiful plain, about fifteen miles up the river Tiber, are the hills upon which Rome was built. In early times, the people who lived in Rome went out in the daytime and tilled the plain, and at night returned to Rome in order that they might be protected. From this it would seem that there were enemies near, would it not? Do you think they were wise in choosing such a place for their city? Indeed it was a very wise choice, because from the hills they could overlook their farms, see enemies coming, and protect themselves; and the river too was at hand, upon which they could sail thirty miles or so above Rome and get the products, and then float them out to sea, and work up a good trade with the people living on the Mediterranean.

At first in Rome all land and trade and wealth were owned by the rich people alone, but in time the poor people came to have little farms of their own, which they lived upon and cultivated. I say little farms, but you will be surprised when you know just how small they were. Could you imagine any one with a family living upon a farm of only three or four acres, or about three times the size of the usual school square? Well, the father of the little Roman boy Marius lived on just such a farm. It lay favorably on a gently sloping hillside facing the east, for there the early sun shone upon it. It had a sandy soil which was easily drained, and it was surrounded by a hedge of trees.

The little farm had its vineyard, and Marius enjoyed going about it with his father, trimming branches here and there, for he knew that the wine of the grape made a large part of their living. He watched the olive orchard as it grew, and in the proper season helped his father to press the oil from the olive. The Romans were very fond of olives, and the oil served them as butter.

Marius, of course, could merely help in the things that I have mentioned, but there was one thing that he and his little brother could do alone, and that was to tend the garden patch, which, to be sure, was not very large, but sufficient, if well tended, for the father, mother and four children,—for Marius had two sisters and a brother also. Do you think a family of six could have many luxuries, making a living on a four-acre farm?

While the father plowed the ground with a rude plow made from a forked sapling, and the mother and sisters looked after the broods of chickens and geese, Marius and his brother carefully tended the patches of lettuce, turnips, onions, cabbage, carrots and many other things which you see nowadays growing in the gardens in the United States. Marius was not yet old enough to follow the plow, but he had helped his father select the tree from which the plow was made, and watched his father make it, so I am sure he could tell you just how it was made. It was very simple, and yet it seems a little strange to us who never think of making our own plows. But the early Roman farmers, having no manufactories, had to make all their plows by hand; and no matter how poor they were, they could have as many plows as they wished, for all they had to do was to hunt a branched sapling, and sharpen the branch into a long point. This served as a share, to run in the ground, and about midway of the longest part a handle was fastened; to this longer part was hitched an ox to draw it. Do you think these plows were as good as those made in our own manufactories of today? No, they were nothing but sharpened wooden sticks, and besides being very poor for turning the soil, they were hard to sharpen and soon wore dull again.

The soil for the wheat, rye and millet was plowed with this plow, and when the grain was ripe, it was threshed by walking oxen over it; the chaff was separated from the grain by flinging it into the air and letting the wind blow it away. After grinding the grain between two stones, arranged much as our coffee mills are, it was mixed with water and was then ready to eat. We should hardly think we could eat it without baking, but the Romans did not learn to bake their bread until a good many years after Rome was settled.

The principal buildings on the farm were Marius' home, and, a little apart from it, the sheds, granaries and coops which surrounded the open court, and in which the hay, grain, wine, oil and broods were stored and kept. Bees had a home here, too. The Romans had no sugar, so Marius ate honey in the place of sugar.

It would not do to forget the flock of sheep which Marius helped drive down to the river and wash off, after which he watched his father cut the great fleece, which the mother and sisters wove by hand into clothing.

This was the time that Marius most enjoyed, for it was then that his father told him many things that his father had told to him. The story that Marius loved best was how Rome, the city on the hills a short distance away, was thought to have been founded. I must first tell you that nowadays scholars know that the Romans just imagined some of the things they told about early Rome; and while we do not believe every story they told, they did, and I will tell you the story of the founding of Rome just as Marius used to hear it from his father.

A wicked king, named Amulius, ruled in Alba Longa, a city a little southeast of where Rome was afterward built. He had robbed his elder brother of the kingdom and killed his brother's sons. But there was a daughter named Rhea Silvia left, and fearing lest she should marry and have sons, who would take back the kingdom of her father, he made her priestess of Vesta. A Vestal virgin or priestess of Vesta was a maiden who watched and kept the sacred fire always burning in the temple of Vesta. You see, the Romans, as well as the Egyptians, Phœnicians and other people we have studied, used fire in their worship. These Vestal maidens were not allowed to marry, but the god Mars married Rhea Silvia, and she gave birth to twins, Romulus and Remus. When Amulius heard this, he ordered the babes to be thrown into the Tiber, and they floated down the stream until they were washed ashore near the place where Rome was afterward built. Here they were nursed by a wolf, and afterward were found and brought up by a shepherd. When they had grown up, they were made known to their grandfather, whom they restored to the throne by slaying the wicked Amulius. They then determined to build a city on the Tiber, near where they had been saved.

You see, the wild life they had lived made them fierce and strong, so they quarreled about whose city it should be, and Remus was killed in the quarrel. Then Romulus built the city, and called it Rome after his own name. He was its first king, and he made his city great in war. He selected old men called senators to advise and help him govern, and these made up the senate; only the sons of these first men, and then their sons, and so on down, could become senators and hold other offices in the state, and you will find later that this brought on a great deal of trouble.

After Romulus had reigned thirty-seven years, he was taken up to heaven by his father Mars, and the Romans worshiped him as a god.

As was said, Romulus made his city great in war. Now fighting makes people fierce and rough, so when wise and good Numa became the second King of Rome, he thought his people ought to be made peace-loving and taught lessons of religion; for this reason he turned their attention to the worship of the gods rather than to war.

Whenever there was war, the gates of the temple of Janus were open, so that the people could go in and pray. Janus, I must tell you, was the god of Beginnings, and I am sure you can guess where we got our name for January. He had a double face, and thus could look backward or forward; but in Numa's reign he was no longer seen, for during the thirty-nine years of Numa's rule Rome was without war, and moved along in perfect happiness.

Numa also appointed priests, who were to dance and sing through the street in a procession once a year, carrying the twelve sacred shields. During a famine in Rome the god Mars is said to have dropped a shield from heaven as a sign of protection to Rome. Numa then had eleven others made, which looked exactly like this one, so that if any one attempted to steal or destroy the sacred shield, he could not tell it from the others.

Because Numa was so wise and good, and taught the people how to worship the gods, they believed he talked with a goddess, Egeria, who told him what was best for his people and how they might please the gods. Egeria led him through the sacred groves, told him how to consult the gods by the lightning and the flight of birds; and so much did she come to love him, that when he died Egeria melted away in tears into a fountain.

There were five other kings, the last being Tarquin the Proud, who ruled very harshly; he was a warrior and made Rome more powerful among the surrounding people, but at last the Romans could endure him no longer, so they rose against him, and drove him and his family out. They then elected, to serve for a year at a time, in place of the king, two men, called consuls. The consuls were to preside over the senate, and lead the army in battle. If in war the state was in great danger and the consuls were likely to be defeated, they could elect a dictator who could rule Rome without asking consuls, senate or anybody else, but who could serve no longer than six months. When King Tarquin was driven out, he went to Porsena, the king of the country north of Rome, and persuaded him to lead an army against Rome, and place him—Tarquin—again on the throne. The news soon reached Rome that the enemy had captured Janiculum, a hill just across the Tiber from the city. A bridge had been built by the Romans from Rome to this hill, and so they feared that Porsena with his army would soon cross and take their city. Horatius, with two brave companions, crossed the bridge to the Janiculum side, and forced the enemy back until the people in Rome could cut down the bridge behind the brave boys. As the bridge tottered and was about to fall, Horatius' companions rushed back and reached Rome just as it fell; but brave Horatius stood until it went down, with thirty thousand foes before him and the great river behind. He then turned and said:—

"Oh, Tiber! Father Tiber,
To whom the Romans pray,
A Roman's life, a Roman's arms,
Take thou in charge this day,"

and then he plunged headlong into the stream. The enemy on one side, and his friends on the other, were silent with awe at such great bravery; and when he reached the shore, he was received with great rejoicing, and

"They gave him of the corn-land,
That was of public right,
As much as two strong oxen
Could plow from morn till night;
And they made a molten image,
And set it up on high,
And there it stands unto this day,
To witness if I lie."

Rome had many such brave men. Do you think such people were likely to be conquered? These stories the Romans believed and loved to tell, and I am glad they have come down to us, too. As I told you, they contain truth and fable and fancy, all mixed together, but the

Romans believed them so firmly that they were influenced by them almost as much as if they had been entirely true. They made the Romans a brave, obedient, patriotic people,—in fact, I know of none who were ever more so.

At first Rome was only a few houses upon a hill, near the river; it grew in numbers, because men came to live within its mud walls, to be safe from their enemies and to trade; and as it grew in numbers it grew in power, until the mud wall, which at first surrounded only one hill, was changed to a stone wall surrounding six others lying near; and thus Rome became known as the City of Seven Hills.

Some of the men were merchants and went up and down the Tiber River in their boats, but the greater part of the people at this early time were farmers, who tilled the land which lay about the city, and from which their principal supply of food came. When you think of Rome, therefore, in early times, you must always understand it meant both the city and the land around it.

It was on one of these farms close to Rome, as I told you, that Marius lived. He not only hears these stories from his father, but he and his little neighbor Cato often talk about them. Only yesterday Cato told Marius that his oldest brother was one of the priests who carried the sacred shields, and that next year his sister would be eight years old and was to become a Vestal virgin, and that then he would hardly ever see her. Marius wondered why one of his sisters had never been a priestess of Vesta, for he thought it must be very delightful to be dressed in white robes and snowy linen in the great temple and keep the fire burning upon the altar, carry the sacred water from the fountain of Egeria and thus to serve the sacred goddess; he often hoped, too, when he became a man that he might be one of the priests. Other things about him often brought questions to his mind and longings to his little heart. The farm of Cato's father was much larger than their own, and Cato and his father had several slaves to do their work. One of the slaves often told Cato many stories, and taught him to write on a waxen tablet with a stilus; and thus he was being educated, and Marius was not. Cato's father sometimes took him to the senate, where he saw the senators in their white woolen togas, or cloaks with purple hems. Marius had been to Rome with his father and had been in the busy market place, or forum, a number of times; he had seen and worshiped in the temple of Mars, for Mars was the god who kept off sickness from the cattle and sheep and kept the grain from blight and disease; he had seen the temple of Minerva, and prayed to her often, for she was the goddess who gave wisdom to all; but Marius had never visited the senate, and he wondered why his father had not taken him there, too.

That night he asked his father why he did not have slaves as Cato's father had, and if he might, when he was a man, go to Rome and be one of the priests,—for Cato's elder brother was one,—and if he would take him to visit the senate. His father then told him that when Romulus chose the senators, there were only a few families in Rome, and that the senators were the heads of these old families. But as Rome grew, many new people came there to live and trade who had no place in the old families, and so had no share in the government. But that was not all: these old families, or patricians, as they were called, thought that because they were older they were better, and so looked down upon those who came later. "They have done this for years," said his father, "and still they expect us to fight when the rough plunderers come down from the mountain regions in search of booty, drive away our flocks and herds, take our grain, and burn and ruin our farms; and yet for all this fighting we receive no pay. The land we get by war the patricians alone use for pasturing their sheep and cattle: that is why our neighbor has wealth and luxury and a large farm, and slaves to do the work upon it.

"Only a few years ago," he continued, "the plebeians were treated so badly that they marched out of Rome in a body, to the Sacred Mount not far from Rome, where they thought they would make a city for themselves and let Rome fight her own battles; but the patricians promised, if they would come back, that the plebeians might have officers, called tribunes, to protect them from wrong. These tribunes left the doors of their houses open day and night, so that any who sought refuge might find it in their homes; and the patrician senate agreed, also, that the tribunes might stand at the door of the senate and forbid the passage of any law which would oppress the poor people. We are still struggling for our rights, my boy, and I hope by the time you are a man things will be so that you may be a priest, but now only the patricians can be selected; and now you know also why you have never visited the senate."

The father told Marius all this, but he did not tell him what would happen if the mountaineers should come down upon them and destroy their crops, and attack the valley farmers and then Rome. But Marius was soon to know. Only the next week, not long after harvest, messengers were sent by the Roman consuls out among the Roman farmers to summon to Rome all men who were able to fight. One of the consuls then led them to battle against the people who lived in the surrounding mountains, but not till the army, which had gathered at Rome, went to the temple of Mars and offered sacrifices and asked the help of the god whom they thought went always before them in battle. Marius' father offered wheat to Mars for the protection of the cattle, fields and flocks, and a measure of barley to Vesta for the safe-keeping of his wife and children, and departed for the war. He was gone several months, and in spite of the fact that Marius and the rest of the family worked faithfully on the little farm, offered sacrifices each day on the hearth-stone to Vesta and Mars, to protect their father, their home and their crops, when the father returned his farm had been overrun and plundered by the rude shepherds and mountaineers who swept down from the upland hollows, buildings were destroyed, fields laid waste, and the little herd of sheep and goats driven away. But the father, who had fought so bravely in the war, struggled yet more bravely to support his family and save his little farm. In order that the family might have food and clothing when winter came, he was compelled to borrow money from a wealthy patrician; for as I told you, he received no pay for serving in the army, and since his crops and stock had been stolen, he must borrow money or see suffering and disease come to his wife and children. This threw him in debt, and his little farm did not grow enough for him ever to repay it.

Do you begin to see how impossible it was, with wars and robbers and little farms, for the early Roman plebeians to keep free from debt? Well, as time went on, what do you suppose happened to Marius' father? By so much service in the army, and by frequent destruction of his crops, all his struggles, and the help of his noble little son, were not sufficient to enable him to pay the patrician from whom he had borrowed the money. His farm was at first taken from him, and finally the father himself thrown into prison. In those olden times each patrician house had its own prison in which to punish the poor people who could not pay their debts. Another hardship for the plebeian arose from his ignorance of the law. What would you think if parents or teachers never told you plainly and clearly what was the proper thing to do, and yet punished you if you did not do it? You would of course think that very wrong. Well, you will sympathize with the plebeians of early Rome then, for this is the way the patricians treated them. The patricians had teachers and had been taught the laws when they were children, but they had never allowed the plebeians to know what the laws were, because by keeping the plebeians ignorant, the patricians could punish them for anything they wished, or take their property from them and say it was the law. But the plebs kept struggling to work out some way to know the law; for, they said, "How can we obey the law unless we know what it is?"

After a struggle of ten years, ten men were appointed to write down the laws of Rome. Before this the laws had been told by father to son. Do you suppose when the laws were written they were written on paper and printed in newspapers? Not at all; for there was then in Rome neither writing-paper, nor newspapers, nor scarcely any books. These laws were placed in the Forum, where every man and boy went very often to trade and attend to other things, and thus could learn them. They were written on twelve bronze tablets, and were called "The Twelve Tablets of the Law." It was a very great help to the plebeians to get these laws all plainly written out. Some of these laws were very similar to those we have today, but one like this we should think very strange: a man had control over his wife and sons and daughters (until they were married), and could sell them if he chose.

The struggle between the patricians and the plebeians lasted about four hundred years from the founding of Rome, until step by step the plebs were victorious, and stood equal in every way with the patricians. They could be senators, consuls, or priests, and finally little plebeian girls could become Vestal virgins as well as patrician. So, while I do not think Marius ever got to be a priest, he probably lived to see his son one.

Often while this struggle was going on within Rome herself, there were other wars, as I have been telling you, with the Æquians, Volscians, Etruscans, Samnites, and other mountain tribes, living north, east and south, but Rome was conqueror over all; for in the long struggle among themselves they had learned obedience, self-control and courage, and by learning to rule themselves had learned to rule others.

As we go on with our work I will tell you about these different wars,—first, about the Dictator, Cincinnatus, and then how bravely the Romans defended the citadel when the fair-haired Gauls came from the North against them, and how the Samnites fought and were overcome, and how, after holding out for some time, the Greek cities along the southern coast were taken, and their Grecian leader Pyrrhus, with his elephants, driven away. But I must now tell you a little about how Rome governed this great "Boot Country," which she had gained through these wars. I have briefly told you how, when she conquered a people, say the Samnites, she would take part of the land and send some of the citizens of Rome to live upon it, and form a little state among the people, which became like Rome. The wild uncultivated people living around these "little Romes," so to speak, were greatly influenced by the citizens from Rome, and gradually adopted their language, customs and institutions, until all Italy gradually became like Rome. Rome made it easy to govern these conquered people in another way. She built great roads. Let us see how these were made: First it was decided where the road should run—over the plains, through the hollows and over the hills. Then the breadth, which was enough for four horses abreast, was laid out by cutting wide trenches. In digging the trenches, earth was thrown out until solid ground was reached, so that the foundation would be firm; then there was placed in the trench a layer of small stones; next, on top of this, broken stones cemented with lime; then, as a third layer, a mixture of lime, clay and beaten fragments of brick and pottery; and finally, as a fourth and last layer, a mixture of pounded gravel and lime, or a pavement of hard flat stones.

These roads were built in all directions to different parts of Italy, from Rome, until they looked like a great spider web, with Rome as a spider in the center, catching everything and drawing it into its power. When Rome conquered a new country, the roads were always extended into it. You see, by means of these highways Rome could send soldiers quickly where they were needed, for the roads were never out of order; and notwithstanding she had no newspapers, and of course no railroads, it is astonishing how quickly messages or troops could be sent from one end of the country to the other.

Thus you have seen how the town of Rome, starting as a little village of mud huts on the Tiber, gradually spread over the Seven Hills and along the river banks and out over the plain, growing richer and stronger all the time, and by her struggles at home between plebeians and patricians, learned lessons of courage, patience and perseverance. After this, Rome, having learned these lessons, was able to go out and conquer all the hill and mountain peoples and teach them to obey her. When Rome had done all this, she was strong enough to conquer the greatest enemy she ever had. This was Carthage; and we shall soon see how she did it, and as a result became master of the whole Mediterranean Sea.

THE STRUGGLE BETWEEN ROME AND CARTHAGE

WE have now seen the little city of Rome, beginning as a few mud huts on a single hill, increase in size and power till it came to rule the whole peninsula of Italy. As Rome's power grew southward she met another great city, on the southern coast of the Mediterranean,—a city so strong and so rich that the wealthy traders in Rome, the Roman senate, and even the plain farmers in the country regions throughout Italy, grew jealous of it and spent much of the time for more than a hundred years (264 B.C.–146 B.C.) in conquering and destroying it. I must now tell you how this city was founded, how it grew rich, and how it fought against Rome for its very life.

You remember that earlier we studied about King Hiram's country, the country of the Phœnicians? Many times we saw those brave sailors push out from their rocky and mountainous shore and start out on their ships. All the time since we first saw them, down to the time when they began to fight with Rome—fully five hundred years—the Phœnicians have been colonizing and planting trading-posts wherever they have gone. A long time ago, about a hundred years before Rome was founded, they established a little trading-post on the northern coast of Africa, far away from their own home country; and this little town grew rapidly till it came to be as large a city as Rome itself. It is now, 264 years before Christ was born, the largest Phœnician city in the world. Since Tyre was destroyed, as you remember, by Alexander the Great, 332 years before Christ, this new city has become the most important Phœnician city, and you would be really right in calling it New Tyre. So now let us take a look at New Tyre, or Carthage, as it was called, and see why it grew to be so large.

Carthage was on the southern coast of the Mediterranean, about halfway between Phœnicia and Spain. For hundreds of years it had been a good stopping place for the ships in their long travels eastward and westward. It was also in the valley of the river Bagradas, the richest grain district of northern Africa. In size it was, at the time Rome declared war against it, larger than St. Louis, and it was a very beautiful city. Its center was a great rock, the Byrsa, which served the Carthaginians as a good place of defense, as the Acropolis did the Athenians. Here were built the chief temples and storehouses, which held enough food for the fifty thousand soldiers who lived there and defended the city when it was attacked. The Byrsa was two hundred feet high. Wherever its sides were sloping and easily climbed, there were thick walls built. North of the Acropolis was the new city, or Megara, as it was called.

The houses and temples of Carthage were peculiar. The people did not like straight lines, so they built their houses or rooms round or circular. They built mostly of stone, made of pieces of rock cemented together with fine sand and lime. The streets were beautiful and had fine shady walks. These were adorned with statues obtained from the Greek cities of Sicily during war, for Carthage fought the Greeks in Sicily very much, and carried home much of the rich art they found there. The Carthaginians themselves did not make beautiful statues and pictures, as the Greeks did. As Carthage stood upon an isthmus, or narrow projection into the sea, it could be easily defended. The city was separated from the mainland by three thick walls running side by side. These were forty-five feet high and thirty-three feet thick. Why did they build them so thick? Well, they were cut up into rooms, and within them soldiers lived. Some also served as stables for the horses and elephants. In fact, within them could be kept at one time three hundred elephants of war, four thousand horses, and twenty-four thousand soldiers, with their armor and all the materials of war. On the walls towers four stories high were built at intervals, from which the Carthaginians could watch any enemy that might come against them. As I have said, these three walls ran on the mainland part way around the city, but one of them extended entirely around, a distance of twenty-four miles, running right along on the water front. Thus the enemy could not land an army in the city from their ships. What a strongly fortified city this must have been! Its massive walls make us think of Old Tyre.

Now let us imagine the harbor of Carthage. It was round, and looked as a great circus would if it were all scooped out in the center and filled with water. In this harbor gathered hundreds of ships from all directions, and of all sizes. There were triremes much like those the Greeks used; there were also larger ships, with five rows of oars, and therefore called quinqueremes. It is said that these vessels could be rowed as fast as our modern war-vessels can travel. How like a swarming beehive the scene must have been around the harbor as the ships went out and in laden with products from all parts of the world. Here were vessels from the eastern Mediterranean. They were laden with linen from Egypt, gold and pearls from the East, frankincense from Arabia, oil and wine from India, copper from Cyprus, and pottery and fine wines from Greece. Here also was a trireme coming in from the North. It had honey and wax from Corsica, and iron from the island of Elba, north of Corsica.

But the quinqueremes had traveled to distant seas—much farther than the ships of any other nation had dared to go. Some came from the Baltic Sea, where they got amber; others from England, where tin was obtained. On the way back they touched at Spain, where they obtained much silver from her rich mines. Other quinqueremes passed Spain at the Pillars of Hercules, the narrow gateway from the Mediterranean out into the Atlantic, and then crept down the coast of Africa, as far as the Niger River. Here they obtained slaves, ivory, lion and panther skins, salt from the salt lakes and salt mines of the desert, fruits, gold and precious stones from the African coast. Carthage took these products, manufactured them into goods, loaded her ships with them, and set out again to trade with peoples in all parts of the world. Now, when we see these riches flowing in from every quarter of the world, we do not wonder that Carthage grew rich, became the mistress of the sea, and, in the third century before Christ, was the wealthiest city perhaps in the world.

But I have not yet told you all about Carthage. Like Rome, she was a conquering country, and after several centuries came to own and control a vast surrounding country. At first, as I told you, Carthage was a mere trading-post. For a great many years she paid rents to the natives around her for the use of their land, because at first she did not wish to own land herself, but was content to carry on a city trade. As time went on the Greeks began to move into their city. Carthage then saw that if she did not keep them out, the number of the Greeks would gradually increase, and finally the Carthaginians would be crowded out, just as the Greeks had crowded out the Phœnicians in southern Italy. Of course Carthage had no right to order the Greeks to stay out of the country about her, for it did not belong to her. But at last, four hundred years after she had been paying rent to the natives, she refused to do so any longer, and took possession of it. Carthage now ordered the Greeks to stay out, and began pushing the tribes about her farther and farther back into the country, and claiming all the conquered land for herself. In this way the nobles of Carthage got immense farms. But after getting them they must get men to till them, for the Carthaginian nobles did not work much themselves. Now you must see how Carthage obtained her laborers.

Let us again follow the quinqueremes as they go on their journeys. Hundreds of them sail westward, past the Pillars of Hercules, and creep down the western coast of Africa. Here at night hundreds of men slip into the negro villages and snatch the sleeping negro men, women and children from their homes, bind them in chains and load them on their ships. Thus thousands and hundreds of thousands of negro slaves are carried into Carthage. They are then sold to the nobles, sent out to the great farms, and forced to work under the lash. It is said that many single farmers owned as many as twenty thousand slaves. So you can easily see how the Carthaginians made part of their money; it was by slave-labor, not by their own. Do you believe these slaves would love Carthage and the great farms as much as the Roman farmers loved Rome and the little farms which they had made by their own toil?

Gradually, as Carthage grew to be a great country at home, she established trading-posts wherever she went, just as Tyre had done. At the time at which we are studying,—that is, about two hundred and fifty years before Christ was born,—she extended along the northern coast of Africa from Egypt to the Atlantic Ocean, a distance of one thousand six hundred miles, or farther than from St. Louis to New York. She owned Corsica and Sardinia; also cities in Spain and western Sicily. You shall hear more of why she wished Sicily after a while.

But I must tell you that Carthage treated the people whom she ruled quite differently from the way Rome at this time treated her subjects. You already know how Rome built fine roads to her conquered cities, compelled them to trade with her, and soon made them proud to be called Romans. The tribes about Carthage hated her because she oppressed them sorely and made them pay exceedingly heavy taxes. For example, Leptis, a small city south of Carthage, is said to have paid $400,000 in taxes every year; and to make a dollar then perhaps required as much work as to make ten dollars now. If any of the cities delayed the least in the payment of taxes, or grumbled, the leading citizens were put in chains, beheaded, or crucified at once. The surrounding tribes were compelled to raise only such crops as Carthage required, and to supply whatever she ordered; no one was allowed to own a weapon of any sort, because Carthage was always afraid of a rebellion; if a village rebelled against Carthage, all the inhabitants were sold into slavery.

You may wonder why all these tribes permitted this so long. I will tell you the main reason. With part of the taxes obtained from her subjects, Carthage hired people to fight for her. Most of her own citizens would not fight, for they were too busy trading. Now you can see if a time comes, when Carthage is unable to pay her soldiers, or if any other country is able to pay more than Carthage, we shall not be surprised to find the people she has conquered and oppressed fighting against her. How different all this is from Rome at this time! The Roman farmers, almost to a man, proudly fought for Rome, because Rome gave them good laws, protected their homes, built roads to their farms, and at this time taxed them lightly as compared with Carthage.

So now you can see, I hope, in your minds as well as on the map, the position of two rich and powerful cities,—Rome in the center of Italy, and Carthage three hundred and fifty miles south, on the southern coast of the Mediterranean Sea. Each is looking with jealous eye toward the other. At the least trifle they will jump at each other's throats like two mad dogs.

But I mentioned Sicily a while ago, and said you should hear more of it. Look again at the map and notice the three-cornered island at the toe of the boot. This island is Sicily. As I have said before, the boot is drawn back as if to kick, and you shall learn before long that the country of Rome really did treat Sicily very roughly. Look at the great Mediterranean Sea, and you will see that this island is almost in the middle of it. It looks as if Sicily is between two large lakes,—the eastern and western halves of the Mediterranean. What a fine stopping place this must have been for the ships in their long journeys from Greece, Phœnicia or Egypt, to Rome, Spain and the islands of the western Mediterranean and far away England! It makes us think of the Hawaiian Islands, in the middle of the Pacific, where our own ships stop for coal, fresh water and new supplies on their long trips to Japan, China, India and the Philippine Islands. Since Sicily had been the stopping place of the Mediterranean ships for a thousand years, it is easy to see why many different peoples would want it and be willing to fight for it. You remember of learning in the previous volume of this series how the Greeks flocked to this island from their native country and built great cities upon it.

But look again at the map, and you will see that this island is not so very much farther from the city of Rome than it is from Carthage. The northeastern corner almost touches the southern part of Italy. In fact it is only two miles from it. The western corner of the island is not much more than a hundred miles from Carthage. A trireme could easily run across between sunrise and sunset. So here are two great cities, one mighty on land, the other mighty on sea, both eagerly eyeing Sicily. Can you see the two hungry dogs, as we said awhile ago, ready to jump for the bone? But is the bone worth fighting for? Let us look farther and see. Sicily is the largest island of the Mediterranean Sea, being just a little larger than New Jersey. But how different its surface is from New Jersey! No land could well be more mountainous than Sicily. In it are no large, flat farms, as there are in New Jersey or Kansas, for example. Indeed there is not a spot in the whole island that is out of sight of a large hill, and in most places lofty mountains are in sight. Since this island is so small, of course there are no large rivers, and hence we shall see no ships on them, as we have seen so often on the Nile and Tiber. There were, however, upon the island many small creeks, streams and springs. During the winter rains these became little torrents, but during the summer they became almost or completely dry.

If we were to imagine ourselves in Sicily during the spring or summer, we should see everything fresh and green, for the slopes of the hills and the little valleys were very rich and fertile. Forests would cover the hills and mountains. We would also find hundreds of orchards and vineyards on the hill slopes. And I must tell you that such an abundance of grain was raised on this island, and so much did Rome depend upon it for its wheat, that it came to be called "the granary of Rome." So rich was the ground that even on the hilly and stony places rich patches of wheat would grow between the stones. Indeed, it is said that one bushel of wheat sown would produce three hundred bushels. No country in the world raised more abundant or finer wheat than Sicily did. Hundreds of flocks of sheep, also, and herds of cattle fed on the mountain slopes. On the southern coast was raised the finest breed of horses. It was here that Rome got horses for her cavalry.

As I told you, the rivers were small, so the ships could not go inland, and for this reason the trading was done at the seacoast. And here it was that the large cities grew up.

One of these cities, Syracuse, on the southeastern corner of the island, was very large and rich; and Athens itself was the only city in the world that was more beautiful.

This island, with its numerous streams, its beautiful valleys, its vineyards, its wheat fields, its orchards of olives and fruits, its fine breed of horses, its herds of sheep and goats, and its wealthy cities, is the prize for which both Rome and Carthage are struggling. Do you think it was worth the struggle?

In early time Carthage reached her arm across the Mediterranean and obtained the western half of the island for herself. Rome, now jealous of the rising Carthaginian power, desired to own the whole island. An excuse for fighting was easily found by the Romans, and the first great struggle between the two strongest cities of the world at that time began two hundred and sixty-four years before Christ, and lasted twenty-three years.

City after city fell in Sicily, until Rome had conquered the whole island except a few strong forts on the coast. These were held by the great Carthaginian, Hamilcar. No Roman general was a match for him. It was now plain to Rome that if Carthage was to be conquered, her great power on the sea must be destroyed. Rome then rapidly built fleets. Soon she became powerful on the sea and beat the Carthaginians wherever she met them. Peace was declared after twenty-three years of fighting, and the great general Hamilcar, who had never lost a battle on land, and had stubbornly held his forts for seven years, was compelled to leave Sicily because of the failure of the Carthaginian ships at sea. Not only was Carthage forced to give up Sicily, with all its riches, and the islands about it, but she was also compelled by Rome to pay the large sum of $4,000,000, which, because money was so scarce then, would be equal in value to perhaps ten times that much now.

Shortly afterward, while Carthage was having great trouble with her slaves, Rome seized both Corsica and Sardinia. When Carthage then complained, Rome compelled her to pay another large sum of money, a million and a half of dollars.

All this was hard for Carthage to bear. Some of her citizens, especially the nobles, were willing, however, to bear it, for they wanted to trade and did not wish to fight. But there was one man who tried to stir his people to fight for their country. This was the brave Hamilcar. And now let us look at his plans. Hamilcar was elected commander of Carthage's army and resolved to conquer Spain. This was the first step in his plan to humble Rome and regain Sicily. For fear he should not live to strike Rome the final blow, he required his little son, Hannibal, who was then about nine years old, to swear at the altar of his god, Baal, to humble Rome and remain her enemy forever. You shall see presently how courageously he did this. Hamilcar then took Hannibal to Spain with him. Here he remained in camp for nine years and became used to the soldier's life. At eighteen he was sent back to Carthage to receive his education. There he became a good athlete, obtained a good knowledge of Greek, and came to know much about the history of the Greeks and Romans, and the great peoples who had lived before them. He then returned to Spain and gained further schooling in the rough camp of war. When Hannibal was twenty-nine Hamilcar died, and the army declared that Hannibal should be their leader.

Thus you see Hannibal was not made general merely because he was the son of Hamilcar. He was, in fact, much like his father in many ways, but he was also the best rider and the best marcher in the whole Carthaginian army. He was willing to bear the greatest hardships in order to fulfill the sacred promise he had made his father when a boy,—that he would give his life to humbling Rome. Oftentimes on the march he slept on the bare ground with only a cloak for cover.

He was ever ready to bear the same trials and hardships that his men did. For this reason his soldiers loved him, and as he never complained of the hard things that came, they too were ashamed to complain.

Soon Hannibal with his brave army had captured almost all Spain,—or as far north as the Ebro River,— and by the products of the rich silver mines of Spain Carthage had gained much wealth. So long as the war did not cost her as much money as they were getting from the mines, the nobles of Carthage did not complain. They were glad to have the land conquered from the wild Spaniards, if only some one except the rich merchants and planters of Carthage would do the fighting. But by all this fighting in Spain an army is being trained for a greater task; for Hannibal, though young, was very wise. He took this as the best means to train an army with which to strike Rome a deathblow. He began by attacking Saguntum, a city on the eastern coast of Spain. This city was a friend of Rome's, and he knew that to seize it would make Rome angry and lead her to declare war.

Carthage did not much like this new action of Hannibal against Rome. But when Saguntum fell, after a siege of eight months, and the rich spoils of gold, silver and fine weapons went flowing home to Carthage, the people rejoiced and declared war against Rome. If the war would continue to enrich her greedy merchants, Carthage would be pleased. When war was declared Hannibal began to make his plans; and when I tell you of the great plan he made you will see something as to whether he was a brave man and a great general or not. He decided to make his way by land through fierce barbaric tribes from Spain to Italy, gaining if he could the help of the Gauls, a people living far north of Rome, up in the passes and around the feet of the Alps. His further plan was to stir up all those nations of Italy who had fought against Rome so long ago, such as the Gauls, Samnites and the Greeks, and get them to join his army against Rome. He could not go in ships, for Carthage, as you remember, had lost her power on the sea in her first struggle with Rome. So he now started out on his long journey, a distance of over eleven hundred miles, farther than from Chicago to New York, before he could reach northern Italy and get help from the Gauls.

Let us take the map and follow Hannibal and see the difficulties he met and how he overcame them. Leaving his brother, Hasdrubal, with an army to watch Spain, he started out in the spring of 218 B.C., with an army of ninety thousand foot-soldiers, twelve thousand cavalry and thirty-seven elephants. At first he marched northward and crossed the Pyrenees Mountains. In doing so he had to fight step by step the wild Spaniards who occupied the mountain passes, and so lost many men. Some of his troops were left to hold the conquered lands, while others were sent home because they were not brave enough for Hannibal. This left Hannibal fifty thousand foot-soldiers, nine thousand cavalry, and thirty-seven elephants, or two-thirds as many men as he started out with.

Now let us imagine how this army looked. There were but few Carthaginians in it, for as I told you, Carthage hired most of her troops of other nations. She gathered them in as she did her commerce, from all parts of the earth. There were thousands of Celts, or Gauls, from the mountains of Spain, who were, therefore, quite used to fighting. These wore a white woolen tunic, with red edges, and carried a shield of bull's hide, a spear and a cut-and-thrust sword. There were other Gauls, in kilts, or naked to the thigh, with their huge shields, a spear and a long, broad sword, which they wielded very skillfully. There were also two thousand slingers and some archers from the Balearic Islands just east of Spain. Nowhere else in the world were there slingers like these. They carried two slings, one for throwing long distances and one for short. They threw both stones and metal bullets.

There were also troops from Africa. Being used to the warm country, they wore but little clothing, covering their shoulders with a cloak, or the skin of a goat, leopard or lion, while their legs were bare. Then, there were the Numidian cavalry of Africa, who were the best horsemen in the world. In these lay Hannibal's greatest strength. The Numidian tribes of the desert went almost without clothing, being covered sometimes with a leopard or tiger skin, and sometimes with a mere girdle of skin around the waist. They used no saddle or bridle in riding, but guided their small wiry horses by their voice or with a slender rod, or stick. These horsemen, always plucky and tireless, were very skillful in the use of the spear.

The elephants were used to charge upon the enemy, whom they trampled down. Towers were also fastened to their backs, and these were filled with archers and slingers.

The army carried along with it but little baggage, for Hannibal had so far to go and wished to go so quickly that he took along but little heavy material. The baggage-train consisted of horses and mules. Carts were not employed till after they reached Italy.

Although Hannibal's army was made up of people of different nations and various languages, yet it was perhaps the best-trained army in the world; for since the first day that Hannibal had taken command, his keen eye and wise judgment had been selecting officers and men who would laugh at the hardships of war and stand like a wall before the Roman sword.

Now let us return to the march. Hannibal had no trouble till he reached the Rhone, a swift and dangerous river, fed by Alpine snows. Here were two great dangers: first, it was a great question how to get the army and elephants across the river, when they had no boats; and second, a large army of Gauls were on the opposite side of the river and threatened to destroy his army should he attempt to get across. Some men would have given up under such difficulties, but Hannibal was neither worried nor discouraged. He bought all the boats he could from the natives and made large rafts himself. While he was doing this, he sent Hanno, one of his best generals, with some troops, quietly up the river to a shallow place, where they crossed without difficulty. When Hannibal attempted to cross, the Gauls faced him in full force, but just then Hanno attacked them in the rear. So surprised were the Gauls that they were completely routed, and Hannibal with his army crossed in safety. The elephants became very much frightened at the floating earth-covered rafts on which they were led, and some of them jumped off into the water, drowning their drivers. The water was not so deep but that the elephants could walk on the bottom, with their trunks thrust up out of the water to breathe. Thus not an elephant was lost.

For sixteen days Hannibal now marched through a rich country of half-friendly Gauls, till he came to the foot of the Alps. Here he did deeds so famous that they will not be forgotten so long as Hannibal himself is remembered. There is no one thing, perhaps, that has made Hannibal famous so much as his pluck and bravery in crossing the Alps, and I must now tell you just a little about it.

One time, as the soldiers and the baggage-train were struggling upward along a narrow mountain-path, the natives, from the heights above, hurled javelins, and rolled huge blocks of stone upon them. It looked for a time as if the whole army would be dashed into the gorges below. But Hannibal restored order, took a position of great danger, and when night came on sent a body of troops above the natives, who came upon them by surprise. By desperate fighting and with great loss of beasts and baggage the gorge was cleared, and the worn and weakened army moved on.

After nine days of cold, hunger and climbing, the army reached the small plain at the summit of the Alps, where the discouraged troops were given two days' rest. Hannibal cheered them by pointing their gaze in imagination to the walls of Rome and to the comforts and spoils soon to be theirs in the sunny plains of Italy. After the short rest, amid the storms of snow, they began to descend the southern slope. This being steeper and covered with fresh snows, made it more dangerous for both beasts and men than the ascent of the northern slope had been. Men and horses often lost their footing and plunged to their death in the gorges below. Once they had to stop for three days to cut a road through solid rock large enough for the elephants to pass along. The great beasts suffered severely from hunger and cold, for surrounded by the great snowfields and ice it was very different from their natural surroundings on the sunny plains of northern Africa.

After nine days they reached the foot of the mountains, ragged, weak and worn. Over half of the army, that is, thirty-three thousand men, had been lost. It now numbered but twenty-six thousand. It was this little handful of worn-out men and a few half-starved beasts that were to be thrown against the gigantic power of Rome, with millions of men for the army and the largest cavalry then in the world. But Hannibal was at their head.

Hannibal's army was now among its friends, the Gauls, who dwelt in the sunny valley of the Po, south of the Alps, and it halted there for food. While it rests for a few weeks and the starving beasts are fed till they are strong again, let us look at the Roman army Hannibal has to meet. Its real strength lay not in its splendid cavalry, but in the common foot-soldier, who fought for his home, his little farm, his gods and his nation. Any Roman citizen from his seventeenth to his forty-sixth year might be called upon to serve twenty campaigns in the infantry and ten in the cavalry.

The Roman soldier, as he marched behind the flag with the "eagle of Jove" perched on top of the staff, looked quite different from our soldier-boy in blue. Besides his tunic (a woolen shirt coming to the knees, bound round the waist by a girdle), he had his implements of warfare, consisting first of his armor of defense, and second of offensive armor and weapons. The helmet, shield, breastplate and greave formed his armor of defense. The helmet, shaped like a cap, served as a protection for the head. It was made of bronze and had a plume of three black or scarlet feathers in it to make the soldier look grander and taller as he went on the march or engaged in the battle. The shield was about four feet long by two and a half feet broad, and was slightly curved, so that it would fit snug about the body and not present a flat surface, easily pierced by the enemy's spear. This shield was carried on the left arm. It was made of two boards of the size of the shield, which were glued together. The outer surface was covered, first with a coarse canvas, and then with a calf's hide. An iron rim was put on the upper edge so that the shield could not easily be split or injured by the downward stroke of a sword in the hands of the enemy. The under edges were also protected by an iron rim so that it might not be injured when resting on the ground. This shield was not found strong enough at all times to resist the flying spears and hurled stones of the slingers in the hands of the enemy, so later the outward surface was covered with iron.

The wealthy soldiers wore an armor about their breasts. This was much like a vest and was made of strips of iron running up and down, which were fastened together crosswise by strong strips of leather. This armor protected the upper part of the body from the swords of the enemy. In addition to this, most of the soldiers wore a brass plate, nine inches square, as a protection to the breast. In a combat with the sword the Roman soldier advanced his right foot. As a protection to his leg he wore a legging, called a greave. This was shaped like the half of a boot-leg split up and down, and was made of metal to fit the front and sides of the leg. It was lined with leather or cloth, so as not to rub the soldier's leg. It extended from the ankle to just above the knee. Sometimes the soldier wore greaves on both legs, for he advanced his left foot when he hurled the spear.

His weapons of attack consisted of the sword and two spears. The sword was worn on the right side. It had a strong straight blade and was used for both cutting and thrusting. Besides the sword he carried two spears, which were his chief weapons in battle. They were almost seven feet long, including the handle, and about three inches thick. The shaft was four feet and a half long, and a barbed iron head, of the same length, extended halfway down the shaft to make it firm.

In addition to these implements the soldier, when in marching order, usually carried enough food to last two weeks, three or four oak stakes to help form the fence about the camp, and several tools, such as hammers and augers. Altogether he carried a burden of from sixty to eighty pounds, and was trained to march twenty miles a day. He was taught to swim rivers, to climb mountains, to penetrate forests, to wade swamps, and to meet and overcome every kind of danger that a life of war could lead him into.

The Romans, always on the watch when they stopped for the night, built a strongly fortified camp to guard against surprises. Around the square camp was dug a ditch fifteen feet deep. The dirt was thrown on the inside and formed a wall ten feet high. Then the oak stakes carried by the soldiers were driven firmly into the dirt wall. These stakes had sharp points at the top, so as to make them hard to climb over. The camp was also strongly guarded by sentinels. So you see it must have been almost impossible to surprise the Roman soldier at night.

The great weakness of the Roman army was in the fact that it constantly changed its generals. The consuls were the generals, and these, as you know, were elected every year. Rome at this time had over seven hundred thousand soldiers ready at a moment's call to fight for her; and so closely had Rome bound her people to her, and so proud were they to be called Roman citizens, that every soldier's breast and heart were as good a defense for Rome as the armor which he wore.

But now let us go back to the army at the foot of the Alps. The Roman army, even if large and well-armed, was no match for Hannibal. He utterly defeated them in the very first battle in the Po valley. Many Gauls then joined his army, and he marched southward toward the Arno River, which had recently overflowed from the melting of the mountain snows, forming great marshes which were thought to make the roadways impassable. But Hannibal had never met a road he could not pass, and after putting his most trusty troops in front, he gave the order to move. On they went for four days and three nights, sometimes in water to the armpits, and sleeping on baggage and dead animals. All of the elephants, as you remember, had been brought safely across the mountains, but now all except one had died from the effects of the mountain exposure or in battle. Hannibal himself, a part of the time ill, sometimes joking with his soldiers, and never discouraged, made his way through the sea of marshes on the back of this one faithful animal. The exposure was so severe that the great general lost an eye from an inflammation which he was unable to attend to. Nowise discouraged by these hardships, on he went southward toward Rome, destroying the farms and doing all he could to persuade Rome's allies to desert Rome and join him.

One morning, during a heavy fog, he completely defeated and almost destroyed the Roman army in a second great battle, on the shore of Lake Trasimenus, eighty miles northwest of Rome. After this defeat Hannibal hoped Rome's friends would desert her. But seeing Rome defeated did not make her subjects love the old city on the Tiber any the less, for very few of them showed any desire to rise in favor of Hannibal. Notwithstanding he was now very near Rome, he dared not besiege it without the help of the people in the country near by to bring him supplies; so he hastened southward, hoping to gain the support of the Samnites, whom, you remember, Rome fought with and conquered about a hundred years before this time.

He thought, too, surely the Greek cities in southern Italy would leave Rome and help him.

Rome now became very much alarmed, and chose Fabius as dictator. Fabius tried a new plan, which was to hang continually at Hannibal's heels and torment him as much as possible, but avoid an open battle. Thus he expected finally to wear out Hannibal. For more than a year this method was kept up, while Hannibal marched about almost as he pleased from one fine valley to another, getting plenty of food for his army and trying to make friends with Rome's allies. Many of the Roman farms were now falling into a desolate condition because the armies had so badly overrun them. For this reason Rome to a great extent had to depend on Sicily and Egypt for her grain.

Once Fabius thought he had Hannibal penned up in a small valley in southern Italy where he could not get out. But Hannibal ordered some soldiers to climb the hill slopes which hemmed them in and drive before them a number of oxen with lighted fagots on their horns. The Romans, thinking they saw the whole Carthaginian army marching off during the night by torchlight, left the road which they were guarding and made for the steep hill. Hannibal then quietly marched out of his pen by the unguarded road.

Rome became impatient of the plan of Fabius, and finally Æmilius Paulus, a more energetic man, was elected consul. He enlisted a large army, ninety thousand or more, and marched at once to Cannæ, in south-eastern Italy, where Hannibal was encamped, with the purpose of defeating him at once. How little they knew, even yet, the strength and power of the great general!

Hannibal met Æmilius on a plain where there was plenty of room to use his cavalry. He formed his men in a line the shape of the new moon, with the cavalry at each end. When Æmilius dashed at him with 76,000 men, Hannibal opened a space for him in the center, then closed on both sides with his terrible cavalry, slew Æmilius, most of his staff, many knights and the whole army except six thousand men. Hannibal is said to have gathered a bushel of gold rings from the dead nobles and sent them to Carthage.

When Rome heard of this great defeat, her people were stricken with the greatest fear and proposed to leave the city at once. It was then that the senate saved the city. Ever wise and brave, even in the greatest danger, it ordered that mourning and weeping for the dead should cease in the city, the city gates be closed, the country crops near Rome be destroyed, so that Hannibal's men if they came might be starved out, the bridges leading into the city be broken down, and new levies of soldiers made. If you would understand this war, you must know that it is the senate, sitting as calmly as a council of kings in the Capitol at Rome, which is guiding every movement in this life-and-death struggle. It was at this time one of the wisest, and most powerful bodies of men that ever ruled any nation, being composed of three hundred trained men who had had the experience of holding the greatest offices of Rome before they became senators. After being elected, they served in the senate for life. They were compelled to attend all the meetings of the senate and were not allowed to engage in any other business. They had charge of religion, the treasury, appointed the dictator, determined what nations should be their friends, ordered the raising of armies and helped in making the laws.

Hannibal won no more great victories in Italy after Cannæ, 216 B.C., though he was victor in many small conflicts. Fabius was again made general of the army, and he tried his old plan. And thus the years went on, Hannibal's army gradually getting smaller through death and because he received very little help from home; while Rome, ere long, regained Capua, the rich city in the plains of Campania, which had deserted her Mistress on the Seven Hills and gone over to Hannibal after the battle of Cannæ.

All this time most of Rome's allies, scattered throughout the peninsula, clung to her like children to their father in time of danger. The Roman traders and farmers loved their country so dearly that they would not give up to a foreign foe, even if they lost their farms, their stores and their lives. Thus you see that when Rome built roads and made her conquered people obey her and gave them just laws and peace so that they could easily trade and become wealthy, she did not do it in vain.

In this way Rome taught the ancient people, and all the world after her, a great lesson. When once she had conquered a people, she attached them to herself by roads and laws, and forts and colonies, and held them as a part of herself in a way that no other nation had ever done before.

At length, two hundred and seven years before Christ, Hasdrubal, the brother of Hannibal, who was at the head of an army in Spain, resolved to go to the assistance of his brother. He rapidly crossed the Alps, as his brother had done, making use of the same rock cuttings and mountain roads which his brother had made eleven years before. Then he hastily gathered an army in the north of Italy and moved southward to meet his brother. Had his plan been successful, it might have been the ruin of Rome; but some of Hasdrubal's messengers, who carried letters telling Hannibal to meet Hasdrubal north of Rome, were captured by Roman troops. The Romans, seeing their great danger, raised an army in haste, and met Hasdrubal and his army on the Metaurus River before they could join Hannibal. The Carthaginians were defeated with great slaughter. Hasdrubal bravely fell in the battle, fighting to the last. His head was cruelly sent to Hannibal and thrown over the lines into his camp. When Hannibal saw it, he sadly remarked, "I recognize in this the doom of Carthage."

Although Hannibal had now lost all hope of conquering Rome, he yet for four years remained in the mountains of southern Italy, holding his army together as it slowly grew smaller. But Rome now chose a new general, who made a new plan to capture Hannibal. This general was the famous Scipio, and his plan was to cross the Mediterranean and attack Carthage. He now raised an army and sailed from southern Italy across the sea to attack the great city.

Hannibal was immediately recalled home by the Carthaginians to defend his country. With a new army he met the troops of Scipio on the plains of Zama, south of Carthage, and for the first time in his life the great Hannibal suffered defeat. Twenty thousand of his men were slain, and he barely escaped with his own life.

The war was now closed, 202 B.C., and by it Rome had gained Spain and the islands of the Mediterranean Sea. She also made Carthage give up her war elephants, destroy all her ships of war except twenty, and promise to pay to Rome $240,000 each year for fifty years.

Amid all these troubles Hannibal did not give up to discouragement. When the war closed, he was placed at the head of Carthage; and so wisely did he rule that the triremes and quinqueremes were soon again pouring the riches of the seas into her lap and raising before her the vision of being mistress of the seas.

But as Carthage rose again in strength, Rome's jealousy rose also, and especially her jealousy of Hannibal. The nobles of Carthage and Roman spies hatched evil reports against him; after seven years of noble effort he was forced to leave his city, his house being leveled to the earth and all his property seized. Hunted almost like a beast for the next twelve years, he fled from one country to another to escape the cruel hand of his enemies. How the Romans would have liked to have him walk in chains in one of their great triumphs! Finally, in 183 B.C., when he was perhaps sixty-six years old, to avoid capture and so great a disgrace, and being betrayed by a king of Asia Minor to whom he had fled for protection, Hannibal took poison, fighting, as he had sworn, to the last hour of his life against Rome or Rome's allies. In the same year (183 B.C.) died his great conqueror, Scipio Africanus, also an exile and full of bitterness toward the country which he had saved when it tottered under the heavy blows of Hannibal.

But Rome was still afraid new Hannibals might be born, and in 146 B.C. made an excuse for fighting Carthage again, and in order to destroy her trade, ordered the Carthaginians to remove the city ten miles inland. How this must have stung and vexed these brave seamen, who had grown rich on the seas for six hundred years! Of course they refused, and then began a four years' siege of their beautiful city.

I have already told you something of the mighty walls which surrounded Carthage, and of the great towers for protection which were built upon them; and I must now tell you something of the implements of war which Rome attacked them with in her stubborn siege. The battering-ram was principally used to destroy the walls. It was made of the trunk of a large tree, and was often one hundred feet long. On the end of it was fastened a large piece of iron or bronze, shaped like a ram's head. This huge log was swung by ropes or chains from a beam above, so that the soldiers did not have to hold it up while they swung it backward and forward, making the iron head go crashing against the stone wall. The beam was made long, so that it would reach across the ditch, fifty to seventy-five feet wide, which was just outside the wall. A roof was built above the battering-ram, so that the men, oftentimes a hundred or more, who were running it, could not be hurt by the weapons of the enemy on the walls.

The Romans also had huge machines called catapults, used for hurling large stones, weighing from fifty to three hundred pounds, over the walls into the city. These they used instead of cannon. Why did they not use cannon and cannon balls as we do now?

They had also high towers built on wheels, which were rolled up to the walls. The enemy in the city could prevent them from climbing on top only by throwing stones down on them, or hot oil, or by digging mines under the towers, so they would fall over, or by some means setting fire to them, or by building their walls still higher than the tower.

Well, as I told you, Rome surrounded Carthage and began the siege. At first the Carthaginians were in despair, but they asked the Romans to give them thirty days of peace in which to consider whether they would surrender or not.

In these thirty days the whole city was turned into a workshop. Lead was torn from the roofs of the houses and made into balls for the slingers. Iron was stripped from the walls of the buildings to be beaten into swords; the women cut off their hair to be twisted into ropes for the catapults and for strings for the bows; stones were piled on top of the walls to be thrown down on those who should attempt to climb them. Oil was brought to the walls, and kettles for boiling it. When the thirty days were over, and Scipio (the grandson of Hannibal's conqueror) came to demand the surrender of the city, he was surprised to find the gates closed and everything ready for the siege.

Again and again did Scipio assault the city, only to be driven back. The rams battered against the walls, but the Carthaginians hung great sacks of earth down in front of them and thus broke the shock. Those who attempted to scale the walls were scalded with boiling oil dashed down by those who defended from the towers above. Mines were attempted under the walls, only to be stopped by countermines dug by the Carthaginians. So, for four weary years full of suffering, the siege went on, the Romans pressing closer and closer, the Carthaginians, defending themselves with heroic courage, but every day coming nearer to the point of starvation. Disease, death and famine began at last to weaken the strong defense of the great city. Finally the walls were scaled, the Romans entered and began making their way toward the great rock, Byrsa, of which I have already told you.

In this last hour of despair the Carthaginians heroically defended every foot of street, every house, every temple. For seven days the Romans fought from house to house, from story to story, till at last they came to the towering rock, upon which was seated the sacred temple, defended by fifty thousand men. Diseased and starving, these soon surrendered; many, however, preferring death to submission to their great enemy, took poison or flung themselves into the flames.

Then came special orders from Rome to burn Carthage, plow up its site, and curse the ground that no city should ever arise upon the site again.

Thus Carthage, living for six hundred years, and becoming the center of the world of trade and wealth in her day, as London is in ours, was crushed to death by her great rival, and her wealth taken up by Rome.

No people were ever braver than some of her people, and no general in all the world, perhaps, was greater than Hannibal.

But although the Carthaginians were so brave and rich, and Hannibal so great a warrior, it is no doubt better that Rome succeeded in this great struggle instead of Carthage.

Rome, with all her faults, had more than Carthage that was good to teach to the world of her time and all the world since.

Rome knew how to teach people of different tribes and customs to obey one ruler—Rome; Carthage did not know how to build and rule a great nation. Rome was coming, at this time, to care for beautiful things; Carthage cared little for art but greatly for wealth. Carthage still kept up cruel and harsh ways of worshiping their gods; Rome was fast losing her faith in her own gods, but by conquering the peoples around the Mediterranean and teaching them to obey *one government* instead of many, it led them after a while to think of obeying and worshiping *one God* instead of many. Thus, though Rome was often cruel in what she did, she unconsciously prepared the path for greater things.

How all this came about, and how Rome wove her web slowly around every nation touching the Mediterranean, and went on for hundreds of years afterward giving the world great models of government, and how after a time the gentle spirit of Christ silently conquered the medieval and modern world more completely than Rome conquered the ancient, we shall see in the later volumes of this series, as we follow the spread of Christianity and watch the influence of Rome spread over western Europe and in the French and Spanish colonies, even to North and South America.

HOW ROME CONQUERED THE WORLD, BUT DESTROYED HERSELF

WHEN Carthage was conquered and destroyed, Rome's struggle for life was over. For five hundred years and more she had been meeting and conquering enemies; and although she was almost always successful, there were many times when it was not certain whether Rome would conquer her enemies, or her enemies Rome.

In this period of five hundred years, Rome had grown from a little village of mud huts and a few hundred people to a great city of fine buildings and streets, and perhaps a half million people. She had grown in size from a little plain on the Tiber no larger than a small township in one of our counties to a great state extending over most of Italy, all of Carthage, and all of the islands of Sicily, Sardinia, and Corsica. She had reached her strong arm over mountains, plains, rivers, valleys and seas, and conquered hundreds of cities with wealth, like herself, and in the mountains scores of tribes who spent their time in wandering from place to place herding cattle and sheep.

But the one most important thing which Rome had done in all this time was this,—she had taken the snarling tribes and quarreling cities of the entire Peninsula and had taught them the lesson of *strength in union* as the father taught his sons:—after binding a number of sticks together firmly, the father brought the bundle to his seven sons, and offered a reward to the one who could break them. They all tried and failed except the last son. When it came his turn to try, he unbound the bundle, took the sticks singly, and easily broke them all. When the other sons said to the father that they, too, could have broken the sticks by taking them singly, the father replied: "My sons, I have taken this method of teaching you the important lesson that in union there is strength; if you stand together and help one another in life, none can injure you or take from you your possessions; if, on the other hand, you do not unite, but each struggles, selfishly, against the others, you will not only ruin others, but lose your own possessions as well." Of all the nations we have studied—Egypt, Judea, Phœnicia and Greece—not one of them had any such power to bind peoples and nations together and teach them to obey as Rome had. And it was because Rome had taught these many people to obey her, and stand by her, and fight for her, that she had conquered every enemy, and had now, about 150 B.C. conquered the greatest enemy she ever met,—Carthage.

Rome now stood like a young Hercules—master of Italy, Sicily and Carthage, all, as you have seen, about midway in the Mediterranean Sea. If it was desired to conquer Spain in the West it would be easy, for Spain was made up of many tribes who had never been bound together into one strong nation; if it was desired to conquer the old countries of the East,—Greece, Asia Minor, Phœnicia, Judea and Egypt,—it would be still easier, for these countries were now quarreling among themselves, and, like the sticks, when separated could be easily broken in pieces one by one.

Rome had grown so accustomed to conquering people, that when she had destroyed Carthage, and no longer had any great power to fear, she was not satisfied. Her appetite grew sharper, the more she ate; the more she conquered, the more she wanted to conquer. So for the next fifty years after Carthage was destroyed (from 146 to about 100 B.C.), Rome took many of her young men from the stores and the plow and sent them to Greece and Asia Minor to overcome the dozen or more snarling, warring states which had grown up there since Alexander the Great's empire broke into pieces about two hundred years before.

We must now see how Rome did this, and finally see what effect it had upon Rome herself.

The first armies sent into the East were under very poor generals and the Romans were often defeated. The people at last concluded to put Æmilius Paulus in command. Æmilius was the son of the Æmilius Paulus who was killed at Cannæ in the battle against Hannibal. He was a poor man, who would not make himself rich, as many of the other generals did, by dishonesty. Now Æmilius had commanded armies in different places and was a great commander. He did not thank the people for the honor of making him general, but said he supposed they thought he could command, otherwise they would not have put him in the place, and that now they should not meddle with his affairs but leave him to do as he pleased; and he generally did do as he pleased, and generally succeeded well. He was now sent against King Perseus of Macedonia, who was the cause of much of the trouble in the East. At Pydna, in Macedonia, he soon defeated the king's army, commanding it bareheaded and in light armor, took Perseus captive and brought all of the king's country under Roman control. He captured very great treasure here, but being as honest as an old-time Roman, he took nothing for himself.

Æmilius sent home to Rome all the riches he captured, and this displeased some of his soldiers who wanted the gold for themselves. When the senate of Rome wanted to vote Æmilius a triumph, the army objected on that account, but an old general arose and said that he now saw how good a general Æmilius was, for he had won a great victory with an army of grumblers. This reply rebuked the soldiers and Æmilius was voted a triumph.

The triumph was a great celebration given by the senate to a victorious general, and was the highest honor that could be given him. This one given Æmilius Paulus was not the first or the last one given in Rome, but it was the last one given to an army made up of *free* Roman citizens and a very grand affair and so I will tell you something about it.

That you may better understand what the triumph meant, I will tell you what a general had to do in order to be granted one. He must have held some of the highest offices in the government. He must have been actually in command of the army at the time of the victory. The victory must have been gained with his own troops. There must have been at least five thousand of the enemy killed in the battle and the war must have been brought to a successful close. Now the general had to do all these things before he might even ask for a triumph and then he had often to press his claims before the senate quite a while in order to get the senate to vote him the honor.

Let us imagine how it was in Rome on the occasion of the triumphal procession. The city was decorated with wreaths of flowers. The temples were thrown open and incense rose from every altar. Sightseers, in their holiday attire, occupied every nook and corner where one could stand. Seats and stands were placed in the Forum and in other convenient places to accommodate the people. Rome was all alive with sight-seers. The public baths, the parks, the race courses, were swarming with the crowd. Officers kept the streets open for the procession, being careful that the crowd did not get in the way. It required three days for all of the ceremonies of the triumphal procession of Æmilius Paulus.

The consuls, followed by the senate and trumpeters, led the procession, after which came wagonloads of the rare and beautiful things taken in the war. Pictures of the conquered countries and forts, having banners with the names of the towns, were borne after them. This took most of the first day. On the second day came wagons with armor, arms and the spoils of war. After them marched three thousand men bearing bowls filled with silver coins, and still after them, men carrying silverware of all sorts captured and collected from the captured towns. But the third day was the most splendid of all. The procession was led by a body of flute players, followed by young men leading one hundred and twenty snow-white oxen, with their horns gilded and decked with ribbons. These oxen were intended for sacrifices to the gods. After the oxen came seventy-seven men bearing basins of gold coins, and with them marched those carrying the gold vessels that had been captured. Next came the chariot of King Perseus, bearing his armor and crown. His little children with their teachers followed, and then came the captured king himself, dressed in black. After all this followed Æmilius Paulus, the conqueror, dressed in the robe of Jupiter, wearing a gold crown, and riding in a chariot drawn by white horses. A slave rode with him and reminded him every little while that he must not be too proud, for he was but a man. The last of the procession was composed of the conquering army—the soldiers bearing branches in their hands and singing songs. After marching through the streets amid the shouts of the throng, the blare of the trumpets and the music of the flutes, the general, dressed in his sacred robes, rode to the Capitol, slew the oxen, offered sacrifices and paid his vows to Jupiter, and then went to the mansion prepared for him at public expense by the senate.

One of the events of these wars in the East had a great influence on Rome and on her life. This was the destruction of another great city. For some offense the senate ordered the beautiful city of Corinth, in Greece, to be destroyed and burned.

Corinth was a wealthy city and full of the most beautiful works of art, such as pictures, statues and buildings. Many scholars and artists lived there. You no doubt recollect that in our earlier work we found that Greece was a land of scholars and artists, and now I want to tell you how Rome got a liking for such things, and, alas! for other things which were not so beautiful.

The general who captured and destroyed Corinth was named Mummius, who, it seems, was a very ignorant but a very honest man. He had no notion of the value of the pictures and statues which he found in the city. He sent everything to Rome, and it is said that he made each captain agree to replace any of the valuables that might get lost or damaged, just as if it were within the officer's power, for example, to carve statues equal to those of Phidias, or paint pictures like those of Zeuxis (who, it is said, painted grapes so well that he deceived the birds), or those of Parrhasius (who painted a curtain so well as to deceive even Zeuxis himself). Just as these fine things were sent from Corinth to Rome, so many other luxurious and artistic things were sent from other towns taken by the Romans. Indeed, Rome was now rapidly becoming the center toward which everything that was artistic, rich or luxurious took its way. And since the sober, practical, warlike Romans did not have a talent for making these beautiful things, when they wanted to learn about them they had to learn from the Greeks themselves; and before they could do this, they had to know how to talk and read the Greek language. This, as you see, will help the Romans to carry Greek art and culture to the West, just as we saw earlier, Alexander the Great carried it to the East.

Before this it was not common for the Romans to know how to speak or read Greek. Scipio, of whom we learned in connection with the war with Hannibal, took great interest in Greek, as did Cato, who so strongly urged the destruction of Carthage, and the Gracchi, of whom we shall learn later.

After the destruction of Corinth, her people, together with thousands of others of the Greeks, were sold as slaves to Rome. You know that Rome has had slaves for hundreds of years before this time, but they were not educated slaves as these Greeks were. Rome scarcely ever left the people alone in the countries she conquered, but sold the best of them into slavery. We once had, as you know, a great many slaves in this country, but you must not think of Roman slavery as being just like ours, for the Roman slave was generally white like his master, and was only a slave because he had been captured in war.

That you may better understand the effect of Greek slavery in Rome, let us imagine an example: Suppose we were to get into a war with France, and, defeating her, were to capture a great many educated Frenchmen. Then suppose a number of them were brought to the capital of your state and your fathers should go there and buy a finely educated Frenchman to be your teacher, one perhaps who had been a doctor, or lawyer or college professor at home; or suppose he should buy the grown-up daughters of a very rich man for your house servants, or the sons for farm hands or gardeners. Would it not seem strange to have such persons as slaves? Well, it was something so with the Romans when they conquered the Greeks and sent so many of them home as slaves. Thousands of these educated Greeks were scattered among the Roman homes. There were also thousands of other slaves, as Carthaginians, Spaniards, Gauls, Asiatics,—people from all parts of the world,—but the Greeks, because of their education and manners, of which I will tell you later, had the very greatest influence upon Rome. Human beings as slaves became very cheap and very plentiful. You have heard the expression, "as cheap as dirt"; well, once the inhabitants of Sardinia rebelled from Rome, and when subdued were sold in such numbers that the Romans had an expression, "as cheap as a Sardinian." A Sardinian could be bought for fifty cents. At one time it is said that three-fourths of the population of Rome were slaves. As to their influence on Rome let us think of these slaves as divided into two classes, or groups,—the educated and the uneducated. Of course the majority belonged to the uneducated class; we will talk of them first and of the educated last, and this will bring us back to the Greeks.

Slaves on the great farms were treated more like animals than like human beings. The master had complete control of his slaves and could treat them as cruelly as his passions moved him to do, even to the point of killing them if he liked, and no one could interfere.

The farmers had come now, at about a hundred years before Christ, to employ slaves almost altogether in cultivating their farms, with the result that the small farmers were obliged to give up farming because they could not raise produce to sell so cheaply as the large farmers. They then went to the cities to make a living, and often became idle, poor and vicious, and spent their lives in stealing, selling their votes to politicians and begging for something to eat. These, you see, are not the self-reliant, plain, common people, free and independent, with homes of their own, like those we saw in the early days of Rome. They have become a class of beggars, depending upon the rich for their living. This then is one thing the wars and slavery have done—they have driven the small farmer out of the country into the city, where he has become poorer and often a pauper in the city of Rome. Thus some of the Roman people are becoming very rich while others grow very poor.

In the second place, there were so many of these slaves who had once been free that it kept Rome continually watching for fear they would arm themselves and strike for freedom,—as in fact they did try to do time and time again. In 73 B.C. a slave named Spartacus persuaded seventy of his companions to rebel with him. They went into the crater of Vesuvius to make arrangements for their struggle for liberty. Here they were joined by thousands of slaves and robbers. Three thousand Roman soldiers were sent against them, but Spartacus quickly defeated them. This victory caused the slaves, around on the farms and in the cities, to run away from their masters by the thousands, until finally Spartacus had a slave army of seventy thousand men. They captured many of the Romans and treated them as cruelly as the Romans had treated the slaves. They managed to withstand the Roman armies for two years, or until their leader was killed and his followers scattered. Thus Rome was always afraid of her slaves, for as I said, there were now really more slaves than there were Romans.

Again many of the uneducated slaves were men and women who had immoral habits, into which the Romans gradually fell.

But I must tell you also that many of the bad habits which Rome contracted from her slave-class, and which helped toward her ruin, were taken from the well-educated Greeks.

That you may understand this better, I will tell you something about some of the customs of the Greeks before they became slaves. You remember how Greece was cut up by the mountains. These many little city-states were never able to make a single government binding them all together. They finally quit trying to do so, and gave themselves up to luxurious living, study and art. They spent so much time in warring and in trying to turn life into pleasure, that they forgot the worship of their ancient gods. They argued so much and so cleverly about some of their bad habits that nobody was quite sure that anything was really wrong or bad. One group of these debaters, or philosophers, as they were called, was led by a man named

Epicurus, who taught that all people should live for was to enjoy themselves. Epicurus himself was a very good man, but what he taught did not have a good effect upon the people, because it gave them an excuse for doing all sorts of bad things which they would pass by lightly, saying these were for their enjoyment, and that Epicurus taught that whatever would lead to enjoyment was right to do.

Besides Epicurus, there were many other leaders in Greece who taught such different doctrines that the people were quite at a loss to know what to believe.

Now, when these educated Greek slaves taught such things to the Romans it had, among other effects, these two:—first, the Romans became very luxurious and learned to spend a great deal of their time in seeking enjoyment at the theater, baths, games, races and gladiatorial shows; and, second, they lost confidence in their own gods and in what the gods were able to do for them. They gave less attention to serious religious life and more to outward shows and ceremonies, such as regarding the lightning and thunder and watching the flight of birds.

These are some of the unfortunate results which finally grew out of the Romans learning to speak and read Greek that they might know about the pictures and statues and books that were sent home from Corinth and other Greek cities. Of course there were some educated slaves from other lands also who helped to bring about similar results.

Since the Romans are becoming such a pleasure-loving people, let us now take a look at the way they amuse themselves, for we can tell something of a people by the sort of amusements they enjoy.

We must remember what a great city Rome had grown to be. At this time the circuit of the walls of the city was about eleven miles, and as many people lived within these walls as now live in Chicago, *i.e.* more than one million five hundred thousand. Dotted here and there over Italy were many other cities, which had theaters and games and amusements just as Rome had.

Let us now in imagination travel into the city over one of those broad and solid roads which the Romans knew how to build so well. We notice, at once, the very narrow streets. There is a lack of windows in the walls of the buildings, many of which are four stories high. The front doors open outward, instead of inward as ours do. The simple Roman home with thrift and freedom and contentment which we knew before the war with Carthage, has very much changed,—the great mass live now in miserable huts, the great nobles in splendid mansions,

Let us not stop now to see the sights of the streets, but enter at once into one of the great mansions, filled in the morning with beggars, who hang about the owner for their daily bread, and crowded in the evening with feasters, who spend fortunes in feasting and drinking. To understand the true Roman in early days as he was, we must see him chiefly on the farm; to understand him in these later days, we must see him in places of luxury and pleasure. Of all his luxuries and displays, perhaps none surpassed those connected with his feasts, and I must now briefly tell you something of a typical one. It is said the dining-table alone, made of rare woods, cost the wealthy nobles from twenty to fifty thousand dollars. Around these tables the feasters reclined on gorgeous couches, covered with coverlids dyed scarlet, and richly embroidered with figures of birds, beasts and flowers. When all had reclined and were ready to dine, slaves passed around the table with silver basins and ewers, pouring scented water upon the hands of the guests and drying them upon dainty napkins. The table was burdened with vessels of gold, silver and fine earthenware. At each end of the gorgeously furnished room were great urns filled with wine, from one of which cold drinks were served, from the other, warm.

After the hands were daintily scented and the room filled with fragrance, the feast began; slaves hurried here and there bearing costly and rare dishes,—dormice strewed with poppy seeds and honey; hare with artificial wings to resemble Pegasus, stuffed fowls, thrushes with dressing of raisins and nuts, oysters, scallops, snails on silver gridirons, boar stuffed with rare birds, with baskets of dates and figs hanging from his tusks, fish floating in gravies, which were poured from the mouths of four tritons at the corners of the dish, peacocks sitting on nests, the eggs made of beccaficos surrounded with yolks of eggs seasoned with pepper, and scores of other dishes strange and costly. During all this time the music of the harp mingled with the voices of boys and girls, who entertained the guests with dance and song. Sometimes, while the Romans dined, roses were showered down upon them from above. The cost of many of these feasts was very great.

One man, it is said, paid $200 for a single fish, another $4,000 for a dish of rare birds, and another the sum of $40,000 for a single dinner. While a few could live in all this luxury, there were thousands of poor slaves whose board cost their masters less than two dollars a month. Many of the Romans had now grown to be gluttons, and all in all you can see how different these days must be from those of early times, when a great Roman general boasted of making his dinner upon a roasted turnip.

Now having taken a glimpse of their luxurious dining, let us see the Roman in the public bath. Many of them bathe twice a day, and some as many as seven or eight times. By doing so they seek to crowd many days into one, and thus get a greater pleasure out of life. Beggars and rich alike bathed in these public baths. The buildings were built of beautiful marble and were among the largest and most splendid in Rome. There were united in the great buildings, a theater, a gymnasium, and many bathrooms all of which were ornamented within with pictures and statues. These buildings would accommodate from 1,000 to 3,000 persons at a time. The cost of a bath was in some instances about one-eighth of a cent, but in many places the bath was free.

The most common form of bath was taken after exercise in the gymnasium. The bather undressed in the outer room, or perhaps in the warm room, and was then rubbed with oil. He then took a sweat in the hot room and then a warm bath. Returning to the first room he took a cold bath and went back again to the hot room for a second sweat. Finally he was rubbed with oil to prevent his taking cold. The bath over, the bather may now listen to what is going on about him. There is a noisy crowd in the bath. Some are exercising, others being rubbed and kneaded by the servants. At times there are noisy quarrels among the motley crowd of bathers; sometimes a thief is caught, for thieving grew very common about the baths as the poor class increased in Rome. The splash of the swimmers, the noise of the players, the cries of those who are selling cakes, sausages and sweetmeats, the coming and going of every class of person, from luxurious senator to miserable beggar, makes this one of the most active and interesting meeting places for the pleasure-loving Roman.

The dinner and the bath have taken most of the day. On the next day let us start early to the circus to see the races and the sort of people who gather there.

As I have already told you, the common people have been pushed off the farms by slavery. They have swarmed to the city and have now become a crowd of loafers and beggars. All they wish now is something to eat and continual amusement. There are so many of them that the rulers and rich people scarcely know what else to do but to keep them satisfied by giving them what they ask for. The games are not religious, as they once were in the plain and simple days of early Rome, but serve wholly for amusement. There have grown to be so many of these games and celebrations that one hundred and thirty-five holidays in the year are set aside that the people may attend them all.

But we must now be off for the races. The building in which the races were held was called a circus and was made of wood and stone. This one, the Circus Maximus, which means the great circus, was between a quarter and a half mile long and six hundred feet wide. The great building was U-shaped. At the open end were placed the stalls from which the races start. Tiers of seats rose one above the other, as you may have seen them at the amphitheaters of shows or fairs. This great circus seated about two hundred and fifty thousand people—nearly twice as many as live in the city of Indianapolis. Down through the middle of the U was a low wall, around which the races were run and on which the judges sat. Instead of having light sulkies and a single horse, as our races have, they drove from two to ten horses side by side to a two wheeled car, or chariot, such as you perhaps have seen in a street parade, or in a show. The driver wore some bright color, such as red, yellow, green or blue, and the people seemed often to think more of the color than of the driver or horses; and so at the races there arose in the motley crowd parties called the Reds, Yellows, Greens and Blues. These parties became so excited over the success or failure of their favorites that they often came to blows. Let us take one of those hard stone seats and watch the teams all dart at once from the starting place at the open end of the great U into the race and go dashing around the circus. What a noise! The trampling of the running horses, the rattle of the chariots, and the terrific shouts of the people fairly make the great building tremble. We can imagine how the Romans loved a race when we think that they often sat watching them from early morning until late at night. This was all very exciting, but what made it more so to them was that they gambled great sums of money on the races. Fortunes were made and lost sometimes in a day. These are, indeed, very different people from those of the day of Cincinnatus.

But what pleased them more even than the races were the games in the amphitheater. Think of some great circus, like Barnum's, at which you may have been, having instead of wooden seats, seats of stone; instead of walls of canvas, great walls of stone; and instead of two rings, but one great ring with high walls, from which nothing can escape when placed inside. Such was the Roman amphitheater.

The principal games held in the amphitheater were not games at all, as we would think, but real fights between men and beasts. The chief amphitheater in Rome was called the Colosseum. It was built of stone, was 180 feet high, one-third of a mile around, and it would take all the people in a large city to fill it full, for it would seat 90,000. Much of this great building is still standing, and is to this day one of the most wonderful ruins still remaining of the old-time world. The men who fought in the amphitheater were called gladiators. Gladiatorial shows were first given in Rome by Brutus, about the time of the first war with Carthage, in honor of Brutus' father. The fights between gladiators were first given only at funerals, for the Romans, like the Greeks, thought that the spirits of their departed dead liked human blood, and the custom became very common. Later, slaves and captives were trained to fight much as in these days persons are trained for the bullfights of Spain and Mexico. Wild beasts, as lions, tigers and leopards, were often thrown together in the arena to fight. The gladiators usually fought in pairs, with swords or spears. When one was wounded or overcome, if the people in the great audience wished him killed, which they frequently did, they turned down their thumbs, and he was killed then and there; but if he had made a good fight and the people wanted him spared for another, they turned their thumbs up. At one time in the Colosseum these fights were continued one hundred and twenty days; ten thousands gladiators and many thousands of wild beasts were matched and slaughtered for the amusement of the women and children as well as the men. The bullfights and prize fights are some of the things left to remind us of Rome's declining days.

I have tried now to show you how what was once the great plain common people, spend their time in Rome. The little farm has been swallowed up by the big one; the common people have been forced to give way to the slave. They have forgotten their love of country and are happy only when they have something to eat and some games with which to amuse themselves.

The rich and the noble have come to be without religion, have ceased to honor the gods; and the statues of the gods, instead of being objects of worship, serve only as ornaments in baths, parks, circuses and theaters. The signs and omens, which were once sacred, are now scoffed at and have been turned to base uses by demagogues to deceive and oppress the people. Do you see that although Rome has grown rich in territory, she is growing poor in honest, industrious, upright men? Rome is rapidly conquering the world with the sword, but in doing so she is overturning herself by wealth, slavery, luxury and crime.

As I have already told you, there are now in Rome mainly two classes, the very rich and the very poor. But we must not think every Roman has become corrupt and lost all love for his country. There are occasionally persons who see the danger that Rome is drifting into and try to avoid it. Such were the Gracchi, of whom I must now tell you.

Tiberius and Caius Gracchus were brothers and of a noble family. Their mother, named Cornelia, was a sister of the great Scipio, who conquered Hannibal. Their father's name was Tiberius Gracchus. The Romans, who sometimes imagined things, told the story that one day the father found a couple of snakes in his bedchamber. A priest, being consulted, told him he must kill one of the snakes, but if he killed the male, he himself would soon die; and if he killed the female snake, Cornelia would soon die. He killed the male and soon after died. Cornelia then gave all her attention to her children. Tiberius was about ten years older than Caius. He entered the army when he was old enough and by his courage and manliness soon won a place of honor. Many of the common people when forced to leave their small farms joined the army in the field. These people came to know Tiberius well and were good friends of his. Tiberius, although of noble family, became greatly interested in the common people, so he left the army, returned to Rome, and was elected tribune in order to try to help them. He tried most earnestly to remedy the evils he saw. He brought forward a law which was intended to divide out the large tracts of land, occupied by the rich, to the common people, and provide small homes for the poor. Of course the rich objected. But finally Tiberius won the day, and the law was passed. In order to get the law fulfilled Tiberius tried to become elected tribune a second time, which was contrary to the Roman law. A riot took place at the election, and Tiberius was killed. His brother Caius was at the time with the army in Spain. He soon came home and was chosen tribune by the friends of his brother. He took up the reforms of Tiberius. He gained the good will of the poor people by dividing among them some of the lands occupied by the rich, and by getting a law passed which gave them corn for food for nothing. While this pleased the poor it was a bad law for them, because it tended to make them more idle than they already were. He won some of the rich people to his side by taking power from the senate and giving it to them. But Caius wanted to do even more than this—he wished to give all the Latins throughout Italy the same privileges as the citizens of Rome, so that they might all vote and have a chance to hold office. When he tried this, the very people he was wanting to help turned against him, and when Caius sought to be reelected, the common people defeated him. In a riot that followed the election, Caius, too, was murdered, that he might not be in the way of the nobles.

For a long time these two brothers were not understood by the people, but today they are looked upon as two of the great men of Rome because of their efforts to help the poor and to keep Rome from going to ruin. Cornelia, by bringing up her children to be such unselfish, patriotic men, was no longer known as the sister of Scipio, but as the "mother of the Gracchi."

While Rome was having these troubles at home, and spending much time and money in races and gladiatorial fights, she also had armies everywhere—in Greece, Asia Minor, Egypt, northern Africa, Spain and Gaul—all of which were made into provinces of Rome.

She gave these countries peace and good government, and bound them closely to herself by those broad, solid roads about which we have already studied. It is surprising to us how rapidly they could carry news over these roads. We should think it very good traveling to go fifty or sixty miles a day on horseback or in a carriage, yet they traveled twice as far in one day. Think of going one hundred and thirty-five miles in one day on horseback! These roads were to Rome, what our railroads, telegraphs and telephones are to us,—they tied that great country together, and made it possible for it to be ruled from a common center at Rome.

But how shall Rome maintain her great government? The Gracchi, as we have seen, are now dead. The senate, on account of the selfishness, luxury and vice of its members, was becoming less fit each year to rule. The time had now come when it was no longer the noble body it was in early days, or in the perilous times of Hannibal, when nobody could bribe it, and when it was so great as to be called an assembly of kings. One man soon became master of it, and by so doing became master of all Rome. Let us see how this all came about.

A poor country boy, named Caius Marius, entered the army, and without any aid rose to the highest position. When he was a boy it was told of him that an eagle's nest, with seven young ones in it, fell from a tree into his lap. The wise men said it meant he would be consul seven times. He learned to fight under the teaching of a son of the Æmilius Paulus of whose triumph you already know. Marius struggled for a long time from one position to another in the lower ranks of the army till finally his opportunity came. The Roman senate declared war against Jugurtha, ruler of a little kingdom near Carthage, in northwestern Africa. Jugurtha was not easily conquered, and Marius, who was serving in a subordinate position in the army in Africa, concluded to leave the army and go to Rome, and see if he could not get to be consul and thus secure chief command.

Now the common soldiers all liked Marius because he was one of them, eating the same coarse fare and digging in the ditches with them; but the Roman general commanding in Africa laughed at Marius when he wanted to go to Rome to be elected consul, and told him he could go, for he had no idea Marius would be chosen. But Marius, on arriving at Rome, told the common people how he thought he could bring the war to a close in a short time. They believed him, elected him consul, and gave him command against Jugurtha. He found it harder to conquer Jugurtha than he expected, but he was finally successful.

As soon as this war was over another broke out, and Rome was in great danger, so Marius was made consul the second time. Well, this continued till Marius had been chosen consul five times, and it began to look as if he would be consul seven times, as the wise men had prophesied when the eagles fell into his lap.

A great danger to Rome now came from the north-east. A fierce and wild tribe of people, carrying their wives and children with them and wandering about hunting new homes, came through the passes of the Alps and tried to settle on the Roman lands in the Po valley. These people were large and strong, with fierce, blue eyes; and they frightened the Romans more than did the Gauls, who tried to capture Rome three hundred years before.

Marius fought these wild people (who were Teutons, or Germans) for quite a while, and at last defeated them in a terrific battle at Vercellæ, in northern Italy, in the year 101 B.C. For this deed Marius was called the Third Founder of Rome, was given a splendid triumph and was soon after elected consul for the sixth time.

Now, if Marius had known how to rule as well as he knew how to fight, and had tried to right some of the wrongs the Gracchi had tried to cure, he might still have saved the common people. But it was said of him, that he cared to be not a good man, but a great one. He hesitated so long whether to join the side of the common people or that of the nobles, that he lost the good will of many on both sides. At last he became the leader of the common people, while Sulla, a famous Roman general, became leader of the nobles. The two parties, already jealous of each other, began war between themselves. Marius was promised the seventh consulship, and besides, the two generals being intensely jealous, the war was a very bloody one. Sulla's party at first overcame Marius and took Rome. It was the first time Rome was ever *captured by her own people.* Marius escaped from Rome, but thousands of his followers were killed by Sulla. Marius had many strange and trying experiences in his flight from his enemies, being once captured and having a slave sent to kill him in his prison; but Marius looked so fiercely at him and cried out, "Fellow, darest thou slay Caius Marius?" that the slave dropped his sword and ran away. Soon after they liberated Marius from prison.

At last Sulla left Rome to go to the wars, and the friends of Marius got control of the city and Marius came back—master of Rome again. He went about the streets with some soldiers, who killed every friend of Sulla's at whom Marius pointed his finger. He was now chosen consul the seventh time, but lived afterward only a few days. On Sulla's return to Rome he put to death more of Marius' friends than Marius had of Sulla's. You see at this time instead of Rome using her army to protect herself from outside barbarians, she is turned into two great camps led by selfish generals who care not for Rome but for themselves.

Sulla forced the senate to choose him dictator for as long as he wished. He was now in complete control of Rome. He used his power well after all the evil things he had done before. He changed the laws in many ways for the better, and, strange to say, he gave up the dictatorship after some time and restored the power of the senate. Sulla went to his home in the country, passed a very luxurious life there for a time, and died in 78 B.C., his body, by his own request, being burned.

Thus, you see, as Rome has gone out to conquer the world she has grown weaker and more brutal at home. The senate has lost all real power, and one man, as, for example, Marius or Sulla, has gained possession of the government and uses it for his greedy ends. The morals and manners of the people have greatly changed and in most cases have become vastly worse than they were in the days of Hannibal, two hundred years before Christ, and have vastly changed from the simple, sturdy morals and manners of early Rome.

The next great effort made to get control of Rome was quite successful. This effort was made by Julius Cæsar.

Julius Cæsar belonged to the noble, or patrician, class of people, but he was a nephew of Marius, and perhaps this is one reason why he joined the people's party. He was only a boy when Marius and Sulla were having their fierce struggles. At one time Sulla wished to kill Cæsar but was prevented from doing so by the friends of Cæsar. Sulla said of him, "In that young man there are many Mariuses," and fearing his power when he grew to manhood, he wished to kill him while he was young.

Cæsar, born in 100 B.C., grew up as other wealthy young Romans of that day: living a very luxurious life when young, but acquired "learning, taste, wit, eloquence and the sentiments and manners of an accomplished gentleman." He had many wonderful adventures when young which we shall study more in detail when we study his biography. He was the greatest orator of his time except Cicero, and the greatest general of all times except Hannibal. He was the greatest statesman of Rome. At the age of forty he wished to be chosen consul. He had for many years been a great friend to the common people, mixing with the lower classes and furnishing them with amusements and games which are said to have been the most magnificent ever yet seen in Rome. He was chosen consul at the age of forty, and till the day of his death, 44 B.C., when he was fifty-six years old, he was the most powerful man in Rome.

Two other great men,—Pompey and Crassus,—wished also to secure power and wealth through office, so they joined with Cæsar and the three divided the Roman world among them. Crassus was soon killed, after which Pompey was made general in the East, and Cæsar went as general to Gaul—that is, to the country we now know as France. There were many barbaric tribes in Gaul, and Cæsar spent several years in conquering them. While there, Cæsar wrote an account of the wars with the different tribes, and when you are old enough to read Latin you will read Cæsar's own account of how he conquered that country and made it a province of Rome.

Pompey, thinking Cæsar was becoming too great a man, tried to gain greater control than he over the senate at Rome. This turned these strong friends into bitter enemies. The fact was that the Roman senate was very weak and corrupt all this time, and was very easily controlled by any strong man; but Pompey, who was now master at Rome, was afraid to try to rule openly without pretending to ask the help of the senate. He was also very jealous of Cæsar's success in Gaul; so, when Cæsar heard that Pompey was seeking to get all power into his own hands, he left his army in Gaul and started hastily for Rome. He crossed the river Rubicon into Pompey's province, and immediately war began between the two great generals to decide which should be master of Rome and the whole Roman world. The story of the struggle between these two great men is a long one, and we shall hear something more about it in their biographies; but here I will tell you that Cæsar defeated Pompey in several battles and followed him to the East, where Pompey himself was killed. Cæsar was now master of Rome and after some time made himself master of the whole Roman world. He was given several great triumphs by the senate for his various victories.

Since the senate and people had shown so plainly that they were no longer fit to rule, Cæsar thought it best to carry on the government himself. He, however, retained the senate and kept up as well the pretense of consulting it. He took the title imperator, or commander. He was, as I have already said, the greatest general Rome ever had, and he could govern wisely as well as fight.

He did many great things for the Roman people. He tried to check slavery. He planted new colonies. He reformed the laws so as to help the common people and changed the calendar to something the way it is now in our almanacs. He gave his name to one month of the year—July, from Julius. He built many fine buildings in Rome and planned others. He extended roads throughout the country. He drained great marshes near Rome, and thus made new land for settlement. But while Cæsar was doing all of these things for his country he grew to have bitter enemies, who said he was striving to be king. On the 15th of March, 44 B.C., Cæsar went to the senate house to attend a meeting of the senate. Quite a crowd of senators gathered about him, as if to ask some favors, when suddenly daggers were drawn and Cæsar was stabbed to death.

It was a sad day for Rome, for the senate was corrupt and unable to rule, and at first there seemed to be no one who could fill Cæsar's place. Long and bloody wars followed between the different parties at Rome, and from all the leaders that came forward a young nephew of Cæsar, named Octavius, afterward called Augustus, conquered all his enemies and made himself master of the Roman world. The great republic which developed Rome into a mighty power is now dead. The senate, once so strong and patriotic, is now corrupt and selfish; the plain soldiers, once so brave and steadfast, have been turned into plunderers and seekers for spoil. By all this weakness, war and vice, as I have said, the government fell into the hands of a single man, and this was the very thing that great patriots like the Gracchi had given their lives to prevent.

Augustus was a good man and ruled wisely, giving such peace to the Roman world as it had not enjoyed for hundreds of years before; and this peace and order lasted during most of the first and second centuries after Christ. Men during this time had opportunity to think and study and write. Much literature that we now read was written then, as the poems of Virgil and Horace; the writings of Tacitus, the greatest of Roman historians; and those of Seneca, the greatest of Roman philosophers.

It seemed in this peaceful time as if Rome was returning to all the glory and strength of the old-time republic; and because of the quiet of the great empire, the good laws which Rome taught the one hundred and twenty millions of people living all around the Mediterranean Sea, and the many writers of the time, this has been called the "golden age of Rome," and sometimes the Augustan age.

But I have not yet told you of the greatest thing that occurred in the world just at the time that Rome became an empire; in fact it was the greatest thing that has ever occurred in the history of all the world.

In a village of a far-away eastern province of Rome, Judea, was born a child that was to change the history of the world more than Alexander or Cæsar or any other great person had changed it. This was the Christ-child. He grew up to manhood, taught peace, kindness and brotherly love to the people whom he daily mingled with, and was crucified; but his great life gradually came to rule the souls of men more completely than Rome had ruled their bodies. The Roman life, as I have already told you, went quietly on in the empire for almost two hundred years after the birth of Christ, during which time all that was best in the Roman language, literature and law spread around the Mediterranean Sea. No nation had ever before brought such quiet to the world, or bound it together under one single government as had the Romans; but after a while this peace was broken in many ways. Men began to quarrel about who should be emperor, and many emperors were murdered. The rich people grew richer and more vicious; the poor, poorer and more miserable. The races and games were visited more often; Rome became all but a nation of slaves, and taxes grew so heavy upon the people that they could not pay them. All this time, here and there were growing up small companies of people, at first plain people and poor, who had taken up the new doctrines of Christ because it gave them something to hope for after their worn-out lives of suffering and toil.

The Romans did not like the Christians, because they would not worship the emperors as gods, and several efforts were made to kill all of them. One very wicked emperor, named Nero, gave great games at night and lighted his grounds with burning Christians, who had been wrapped in tar and pitch and raised on long poles. If anything went wrong in Rome, as the occurrence of a plague or great fire, the Christians were sure to be blamed for it, and many would be put to death.

Once, when they were having gladiatorial fights, a Christian named Telemachus jumped into the arena and separated the fighters. But Telemachus was stoned to death at once by the people for spoiling their sport. The emperor, however, ordered the gladiatorial shows to be stopped; there were growing to be so many Christians now that he did not dare oppose them.

The Christians were growing in numbers for two chief reasons:—first, the old religion of Rome, because the people had lost confidence in their gods, had ceased to give them peace of mind, while Christianity gave them hope and filled the longings and aspirations of the soul as no other religion could; and, second, the government all around the Mediterranean Sea with fine roads leading to every part of the empire made traveling so easy that people could readily pass from place to place and carry the new doctrine.

Finally, about 325 A.D., a Roman emperor named Constantine adopted the Christian religion and proclaimed it the religion of the whole empire. From that time on all the Roman empire rapidly became Christian.

During the first three centuries after Christ was born, Rome was able to keep back the strong German tribes who wandered through the woods of the North; but as Rome turned more to pleasure and vice, the Roman army was filled largely with German soldiers, who, living for a time in Rome, saw some of the new life there and often took it back to their German homes. Trade gradually sprang up between the Germans and Romans, and whole tribes of rude warriors were hired by Rome to protect her borders; but finally in 476 A.D., a German barbarian chief, Odoacer, captured the Eternal City, compelled the boy-Emperor, Romulus Augustulus, to give up the Crown, made himself king, and, with the force and ignorance of a barbarian, began to rule in the seat which had been occupied by Roman Kings, Consuls and Emperors for more than a thousand years. But what the Germans, or Teutons, as they are often called, found at Rome, and how the Romans finally educated the Germans, just as the Greeks educated the Romans, we shall see in the next volume of this series.

Now let us look back over the great stream of Roman history and briefly review what we have seen.

First we saw infant Rome, nourished, as it were, on wolf-milk, grow to be as strong and brave as a wolf itself. We saw Rome creep slowly out from her seven hills till she had conquered the people near by on the plains, then up to the mountains and conquer the rough, half-civilized, mountaineers. All these people she bound tightly to herself by building permanent roads through their territory, settling colonies among them, and teaching them the laws, manners and customs of Rome.

All of this time there was going on at Rome the fierce struggle between the rich patrician and the poor plebeian. After two hundred years of struggle, the plebeians became equal to the patricians. Rome then felt strong, and with a senate, composed of brave, virtuous, unselfish men, began the fierce struggle with Carthage and her great general, Hannibal. With Carthage conquered, we saw Rome, like a mighty fisherman firmly draw her net of law around the Mediterranean and catch and hold securely in its meshes all the peoples studied earlier,—Egypt, Judea, Mesopotamia, Phœnicia and Greece. All these she finally bound into one immense government, having one ruler, one law, one mighty system of roads reaching to every corner of the immense empire. Then we saw Greek literature and Greek philosophy spread throughout the west. Finally, as Rome was growing old and losing her power to rule, we saw the rise of the King whose kingdom was not to be of this world, and whose law was to be the law of love. As men came to understand this law, slowly, quietly and almost unnoticed, Christianity took root and, amid much opposition, continued to grow till it burst the bounds of the old empire and spread throughout Europe. Rome had lived for more than a thousand years and had taught the world as no other nation had been able to do the great lesson of how to build a mighty nation with a single center from which to rule. In doing so, she had become the great western reservoir which gathered into this center the streams of wealth, culture, art, law, philosophy, literature, religion and learning which had been slowly flowing westward from Memphis, Babylon, Tyre, Jerusalem, Athens and Alexandria through the thousands of years which had gone before.

When Rome died as a government she did not die in the hearts and minds of men, for, as already said, a mightier power than she arose to carry all this thought and culture forward into the north and west of Europe and finally on to America,—this was the great power of Christianity and the Christian Church.

Thus we more and more see, as we go on with our study of the stream of history, how the great things worked out by one nation are not lost to the world when that nation dies, but are caught up and carried on to future peoples and nations by the great institutions of religion, government, industry, education and social life which all people help to work out and which, being continually nourished with new thought, always remain young.

CPSIA information can be obtained at www.ICGtesting.com
Printed in the USA
LVOW12s2311180714

394963LV00001B/56/P